IN HIS
PRESENCE

The Secret of Prayer

A Revelation of What We Are In Christ

★

**A Solution of the Prayer Problem
A New Conception of This Sacred
Privilege**

By
E. W. KENYON

E. W. KENYON
Author

Eleventh Edition

CONTENTS

FIRST WORDS

THIS book is not written about what others were and did, but about what we are and can do!

It is a revelation of what we are in Christ, an unveiling of what He can do through us.

It is a lifting of the curtain and a revealing of the holy of holies and our ability to enter it and stand in the presence of the Father.

It is a revelation of our ability to stand in His presence on the behalf of others.

It is a discovery of God's ability available to anyone in Christ— an introduction to ourselves in Christ.

Much of it will be new and a challenge to earnest spirits to climb the heights and to sound the depths of these tremendous spiritual realities.

It will enable us to know Him and the power and the ability that was revealed in His Resurrection, and the amazing fact that that ability is ours!

It will show us our legal rights in Christ; that we do not stand upon His sufferance or His pity, but upon our legal rights, claiming them for our very own.

It will remove the mist that has surrounded the prayer life, and lead us out of spiritual mysticism into the Light of Life.

It will show us the authority of the Name of Jesus, and how to use it.

It will show us the ability of the Indwelling One in us.

It will reveal our place in the Family and show us how to take that place.

This is not a book of philosophy or of theories, but it is a book of reality.

It shows us what belongs to us and our ability to enjoy all these rights in Christ.

The call to prayer is the Father's invitation to visit with Him. This is more than the consciousness of a great need that often drives us to intercession. It is the call of Love to come and Fellowship. It is really visiting with the Father.

Few of us have realized the fact that the Father's heart is hungry for the companionship of His children. His heart hunger is the reason for man and the reason for redemption, "For God so loved the world that He gave His only begotten Son."

That love impells Him to call us to Prayer.

That call is the proof of our ability to stand in His presence. It is the proof of His making us righteous enough to stand in His presence without reproof or condemnation.

It means that we are ever welcome to the Throne Room.

How few of us have ever realized this.

It is sons visiting their Father.

It is children coming joyously into the presence of a Loving Parent.

He does not demand Faith of His Children. He doesn't say "Now if you believe" or "If you have faith" or "If you love me". He said that to the Jews, His Servants, the men of the Broken Covenant, but He says to us "Come unto me all ye that labor and are heavy laden and I will give you rest." It is the Father's invitation to the Throne Room of Love.

Chapter The First

WHAT PRAYER IS

RAYER is our Need crying out for help.

Prayer is the voice of Faith to the Father.

Prayer is born then of the sense of need, and the assurance that the need will be met.

Unbelief cannot pray; it can only utter words.

Prayer is the Living Word in lips of faith.

It is holding His Word up to Him in prayer like a mirror.

He sees Himself in His Word.

He said it. You are asking Him to do it.

He promised. You hold that promise up to Him in prayer.

You see, God and His Word are One, just as He and Jesus are One.

He honored His Word by calling His Son, "The Word."

His Son, then, and the Word are One.

He was with the Son, and in the Son; so He is in the Word and with the Word today.

When we quote the Word, we quote Him. When we rest on the Word, we rest on Him.

His Word is my contact with Him.

His Word in the lips of faith, is He Himself speaking.

Then we are speaking His Word back to Him.

We hold His Word as a bank holds our note. Just as we have collateral to make the note good, God has ability to make His Word good.

Prayer, then is facing God with man's needs, with His promise to meet those needs.

He taught us to pray. He taught us to trust His Word.

Prayer is a part of God's program for us.

He encourages us to act on His Word. He is one with us in this prayer life.

It is His way of saving, healing, and blessing men.

Jesus said in Luke 18:1: "Men ought always to pray and not faint."

I have two striking translations: "Men ought always to pray and not turn out badly," or "Men ought always to pray and not cave in."

You see, prayer means vital contact with the Father. We are near enough to Him to breathe in His very presence.

Prayer means that we have come boldly into the throne room and are standing in His presence.

It is more than bringing Him on the scene. It is going into the presence of the Father and Jesus in an executive meeting, laying our needs before them and making our requisitions for ability, for grace, healing for someone, or victory for someone, or for financial needs. Whatever that need may be, we are making a demand upon Him.

One day when the crowd was pressing around the Master, Jesus said, "Someone has touched me." And they said, "Master, the multitudes press thee and crush thee." But He answered, "No, someone has made a demand upon my ability." (20th Cent. Trans.)

That is a beautiful translation, and it is so suggestive. There cannot be any touching of the Master without the Master knowing it. When need touches Him, it makes a demand upon His ability to meet that need; and prayer is the way in which we touch Him.

Prayer keeps man in close contact with the Father and with the Word.

It is a constant communion with the Father and it enriches one spiritually.

It illumines the Word, and illumines the mind; and it freshens and heals the body.

A strange feature about this prayer life is that it reaches to the uttermost parts of the earth. When I pray for a man in London or in Africa my spirit can send to him through the Father, the blessing that he needs today. It is the original wireless method.

It is the original radio means of communication.

I speak here, and they are instantly blessed there.

What a ministry!

Prayer Is a Spiritual Exercise

Your spirit is contacting the Father.

Your spirit is reaching other human spirits through the Father.

Paul said, "My spirit and the Lord Jesus will be with you in your deliberations." It doesn't seem credible.

Sense knowledge can't grasp this. It is in the realm of the recreated spirit.

We become so utterly one with Him.

We become so utterly ruled and governed by the Word and by the Holy Spirit that we become Masters of demons and of their work.

We cast out demons with the Word.

We pray for sick folks and the diseases leave them.

Weakness is destroyed by the strength of God.

The very life of God flows out through our lips.

Do you remember John 7:38-39 where Jesus says, "He that believeth on me, as the Scripture hath said, from within him shall flow rivers of living water." 20th Century Translation: "Shall gush torrents of living water."

Jesus is speaking of the Holy Spirit's indwelling presence; and how, from our inner life of prayer, there gushes forth a torrent of the very life of God that speeds on its way to that one who is in need. No one knows about the fulness of this. We are in the very infancy of this prayer life.

Electricity has made the wireless and the radio realities.

Electricity is God's life in the mechanical world.

Will that life in the mechanical world be stronger, more efficacious than His Nature in our spirits? I can't believe it.

I know that our prayers bring the very presence of God upon men in any part of the world.

You see, this is cooperating with Him. God through you is ruling the demons and evil forces all over the world. You become His voice in that Name.

The Word really becomes the sword of the spirit, and it is waging a war against demoniacal forces who rule men.

His Word through your lips dominates these world forces. They don't know it, but they feel cramped, bound, hindered, conquered.

Jesus said, "In my name ye shall cast out demons." That means rule them, govern them.

God through you, then, can sway the nations.

Now you can understand 2 Cor. 6:1: "Laboring together with Him."

How? Through this marvelous prayer life.

You have entered the Holy Priesthood in your prayer life. You can be God's voice, His spokesman, His ambassador, His under-ruler in Jesus' Name through the Word in your lips.

You become God's will toward a Satan ruled world.

You are taking Jesus' place. You are acting in His stead.

Once more God is set free among men.

You remember that God gave to Adam dominion over all the universe. That dominion was restored to us through Jesus, but it is of no value to us unless we, the Jesus men, use that authority in His Name.

That authority was given to an individual, Adam. Now the authority is given to us as believers in the Name.

Jesus exercised that dominion. He ruled the sea. He ruled the fish. He ruled the human body. He made legs grow where they had been amputated. He fed the multitudes.

Jesus did not exercise any authority or ability that is not latent in His Name today.

Some day there is going to rise a people who will take Jesus' place and bless humanity as Jesus blessed them in dear old Galilee.

Did not Jesus say in Matt. 28:18-20: "All authority hath been given unto me in heaven and on earth. Go ye therefore and make disciples, (not converts, but students of the Word,) of all nations, ... and lo, I am with you always, even unto the end of this age."

He is with us in the Word, that living Word.

He is with us in His Name.

He is with us in the presence of the Holy Spirit.

We join forces with Him in this prayer life.

That "all authority" was given to Him as the head of the Church, and it is for the Church to use.

The authority that is in His Name is in your lips. You let that authority loose. You give it liberty and it blesses men.

He has made us Sons.

He has given us the Name.

He has given us the Holy Spirit.

He has restored all that Adam lost and more.

We are Satan's rulers.

We are masters of demons and laws that sin brought into being.

Why did He redeem us? Why make us New Creations? Why make us righteous? Why dwell in us? Why give us the Name? Why say that in Jesus' Name we could cast out demons?

What did He expect us to do after making us all this? Just to be good, neutral sons who never face the enemy; who simply read the Word but never act on it; who do not take our Redemption and New Creation seriously?

Is He mocking us? Is His Word like dry clouds in a drouth?

Is Satan invincible? Must we yield to Satan's dominion and Satan-ruled circumstances?

Must we say that tanks, planes and bombs are to rule the world?

Or is God still living, and are we tied up with Him?

I can feel God's question there. He is saying to me, "Have you taken these facts as seriously as your nation has taken the draft laws? Is my Redemption and New Creation as real as the taxes? Does it mean anything?

We must face this issue.

We are surrounded by demoniacal forces that are dominating the human on earth, and if the Church hasn't authority over these, then no one has.

But the Church has! And prayer is our method and mode of dominating these diabolical forces that are wrecking civilization.

Taking Our Place

Everyone of us has a place in the prayer life.

God has no unused members.

There isn't a useless member in the physical body; neither is there in the spiritual body of Christ.

God has planned with divine wisdom, the body of Christ; and the moment that you are born into that body, you have your place in which to function.

If any one thinks that because of lack of training or for lack of this or that, he hasn't a place, he is deluded by the enemy.

You have a place.

With that place comes responsibility, and with responsibility comes a reward or demerit.

If you do not take your place in the Family of God, in the Church, and begin to function, the body of Christ is weakened because of it.

Some have the idea that their special vocation is to criticize others because they are not doing more.

The Holy Spirit is the *Only One* who has this position.

You have no right to set yourself up as a critic.

Your business is to find your place and fill it.

Until you do, you will pay the price.

I want you to know, my brother, my sister, that the price you pay for staying out of the will of God is expensive.

You may pay it in sickness, in loss of money or in unhappiness with your loved ones; for you can't be the protected one, the cared-for one as long as you are standing outside of the Lord's will for you.

Take your place!

Give yourself to meditation, prayer, and study of the Word.

Don't allow anything to stand in the way of your finding your place.

Life will not mean much to you outside of His will.

The big thing of life is to be in the Will of the Father.

You say, you were never called to give your life in prayer?

No. You may not have been set apart by the Spirit for that special ministry, but I think it would be wise for you to spend enough time in prayer to get acquainted with the Father. Luke 18:1.

There are only two ways of getting acquainted: through the Word, and by Prayer.

If you don't take time to pray, you are losing out.

You can't say that you have no responsibility in the prayer life, for you have.

To see a need is to have a call to prayer.

There are people who will be utterly lost unless you take your place.

Unless you do your part, men will cry against you through eternity.

You can't plead that you have too much work to do. You can pray while you work.

You can't put up the plea that you do not know how; you can learn if you wish.

For you to disobey the prayer call is for you to disobey the call of your Father.

The prayer responsibility today is the most important thing of our lives.

Did you ever realize that there are men and women who are defeated and are breaking down in their business, home and spiritual life because we haven't prayed?

Let me change it: because YOU haven't prayed?

You have been occupied with your pleasures and your dreams; and men and women, staggering under the burdens you should have carried, are breaking down.

Oh, God, have mercy upon us!

As you read this, do not read it simply to awaken you for the moment, but let prayer become like your eating, or your business, or your home.

If you are a mother or a wife, and live at home, there are certain duties which you perform every day for your family.

The greatest duty that you will ever perform for your family will be the prayer duty.

It may be that it is no longer a privilege.

You have thrown the privilege away.

You have ignored it.

It has now become a stern duty.

You must go back to your prayer closet and begin anew your fellowship with Him.

Do it for the sake of your family, the boys and girls; for the sake of your home and church; and God will honor you.

Children are growing up in Christian homes without the restraining power of God over their lives.

The reason is apparent! Mothers and fathers have failed in their responsibilities in the prayer life.

I call on you, men and women, who yourselves are to blame for the crime and the lawlessness of the youth of this generation, to go and ask His forgiveness, and to take up your responsibilities, NOW!

In His Presence

Way back yonder in the Garden the first man lived in the Presence of the Creator, Jehovah Gòd.

He had no sense of unfitness or need of fitness.

He was like a child who climbs up into his father's arms. The child has no sense of fear, no sense of need, for he belongs; and because he belongs, he takes his place, he takes liberties.

But when the great blunder was made, and Adam in a foolish moment sold out his vast privileges and rights to an enemy, he was driven away from the Presence; and a flaming sword was at the gateway to keep him out.

That Garden of Desire with its tree of Life was known to all the people; and for thousands of years, until the flood came, and yet no one could get into the Presence of God.

Then Jehovah separated Abraham and cut the Covenant with him, giving a promise of the Messiah to come through him; his descendants were also given a Law and a Priesthood, and they cut the Covenant with Jehovah through the priest.

God dwelt in their midst in the Holy of Holies.

No one could approach Him unless he was covered by a cloud of incense and had in his hand a basin of blood to sprinkle on the Mercy Seat; and that was only to be done once a year by the appointed priest.

Israel was a servant.

The Unapproachable Presence was in the Holy of Holies.

The heart of man was just as hungry after God as it had been the day that Adam was driven out of the Garden.

The heart-hunger of man has given us all the religions of the old world, all the religions of the East.

It has also given us all our modern philosophical and metaphysical religions.

Man's heart-hunger is one of his most outstanding features, a very badge of the human.

But you mustn't think for a moment that the hunger is all on one side.

God's child-hungry and love-hungry heart created a universe, put in the center of it a world to be a home for His man; and He created man after His own image and likeness, an eternal being; and you know how that man failed Him.

All down through human history is the trail of man's hunger and of God's outreaching toward that spirit-hungry man, until the Man, Jesus, came.

The Incarnation of Jesus is the master stroke of love.

It was God's intrusion into the sense realm where man began to live, when driven from the Garden.

God unveiled Himself to the senses of the Jewish Nation. They had no spiritual appreciation because they were spiritually dead.

Jesus in His earth walk revealed to the men of the senses who surrounded Him, a strange, a phenomenal thing: He talked with God Almighty, the God of the Jews, with a sense of intimacy that they couldn't understand, and finally He called their God, His Father.

To them, that was blasphemy, and they stoned Him for it; they hounded Him until finally they took Him before Pontius Pilate and accused Him saying, "He makes God His Father; that's blasphemy, and He ought to die."

Jesus paid the price of confessing God as His Father.

But before He did that, one day He said, as recorded in John 14:6: "I am the Way, and the truth and the life."

I remembered that Acts 9:2 is the story of Paul's being sent to Damascus with authority to arrest any that he found who were of "the Way."

And then in Acts 19:9: "But when some were hardened and disobedient, speaking evil of 'the Way' before the multitude."

Acts 19:23: "And about that time there arose no small stir concerning 'the Way'."

Acts 18:26 tells the story of how Priscilla and Aquila heard Apollos, a disciple of John the Baptist, who had not yet heard of Jesus, and they "expounded unto him the Way of God."

The same thought is brought out again in Acts 22:4: "And I persecuted this 'Way' unto the death." Paul here is standing before the People of Jerusalem, telling how he had persecuted "the Way."

Paul is again defending himself in Acts 24:14: "But this I confess unto thee, that after 'the Way' which they call a sect, so serve I the God of our Fathers."

These scriptures were puzzling.

Why did he call it "the Way?"

"The Holy Spirit this signifying, that the way into the holy place hath not yet been made manifest, while the first tabernacle is yet standing." (Heb. 9:8)

This began to throw light on it as "the Way" into the Holy of Holies.

But Heb. 10:19-20 clears it up. "Having therefore, brethren, boldness to enter into the holy place by the blood of Jesus, by the Way which he dedicated for us, a New and Living Way, through the veil, that is to say, His flesh."

Now we can understand it.

The "New Way" that Paul preached was "the Way" into God's Presence.

Way back yonder Adam lost "the Way."

Jesus came to point it out.

He said, "I am the Way, I am the Reality, and I am the New Kind of Life."

Now in Heb. 4:16 he tells us to come boldly to the Throne of Grace; that means to come boldly into the Holy of Holies; to come with freedom into the very Presence of God.

Now our hearts can understand Mark 15:38: "And the veil of the temple was rent in two from the top to the bottom."

Josephus tells us that that wonderful veil was four inches thick and fifteen feet square, made of the finest dyed linen, inwrought with threads of gold.

It shielded the Holy of Holies so that no one could enter but the high priest, and he but once a year in a cloud of incense with a bowl of blood to make the yearly atonement for the nation.

Now an angel has come and that curtain is rent, not from the bottom, but from the top, showing that God has been there and ripped that curtain apart throwing the Holy of Holies open; not to the high priest only, but to everyone whom the blood of Jesus Christ has cleansed.

In other words, God the Father is no longer shut in alone.

He can be approached.

He can be met.

But that isn't all. Try to imagine yourself a Jew back yonder under that first Covenant, and you know that no Jew could approach God and live.

Nadab and Abihu were struck dead upon the portals when they attempted to go into God's Presence uninvited. It was upon that great festival day when the priesthood had just been set apart by Moses. Aaron's two beautiful sons lay dead. Lev. 10:1-3.

From that day on no man ever attempted to enter the Holy of Holies except a king. He was struck with leprosy as he entered the Holy place attempting to go into the Holy of Holies, and he lived in a leper house the rest of his life.

For anyone to touch the Ark of the Covenant meant death, as it did to David's friend who dared put his hand up to steady it when the oxen had jarred the vehicle that bore it.

Now Jesus said, "I am going to be the Way into the Presence of the Father. Men are going to be able to enter into His Presence."

Can't you see what that would mean to the prayer life?

Here is the secret of prayer.

We have utterly failed to grasp the significance of the heart hunger of the Father. He longs for our companionship.

John 14:23 gives us an illustration: "Jesus answered and said unto him, If a man love me, he will keep my word: and my Father will love him, and we will come unto him, and make our abode with him."

Does your heart grasp it?

Jesus said: "The Father and I will come and make our home with you."

He is no longer in the Holy of Holies.

The sin problem has been settled.

Man has received Eternal Life, has become His very child.

Now His great heart of love says, "I want to come and make My home with you."

Can you see what lies back of this?

There has been a restored righteousness.

Man has become Righteous.

He can stand in the Father's Presence without the sense of guilt, condemnation or inferiority; and on the basis of this righteousness man has Fellowship.

This is the object, the heart-reason for the entire Redemptive Program.

What would Relationship mean without Fellowship?

God could make man His son, but if that son didn't have fellowship with the Father, then there is no joy for the heart of either.

Fellowship really means "drinking out of the same cup."

It was like our old fashioned communion table where the pastor or elders passed a cup and each one of us took a sip of the wine.

That was a type of communion.

Now the Father has called us into communion with His Son. We drink together.

Can't you hear Him say, "Behold, I stand at the door and knock: if any man hear my voice and open the door, I will come in to him, and will drink with him?" (Rev. 3:20)

Now what does it mean to us?

It means that the last barrier between the Father and the children has been put away.

We may come into His Presence now with the same freedom that Jesus had.

Now we can see what prayer can mean.

It isn't the old idea of getting on our knees and crying and begging.

It is a son coming into the Father's Presence for one of our brethren who has been injured, or for one who for some reason cannot come and make his appeal personally. We come on his behalf and ask for a blessing.

Or it may be that we are taking up the need of the great unsaved world.

We stand there in fulness of Fellowship and fulness of Joy to get a portion for another.

This is entering by the New and Living Way.

This is coming boldly to the Throne of Grace.

This is fellowshipping the Father.

This is visiting with Him.

It is not coming into His Presence as the Jews came into the presence of Jehovah, or as a sinner would approach, but we are coming as sons and daughters.

We are taking our place.

1 Peter 2:3-5 gives us a picture of our Holy Priesthood. "If ye have tasted that the Lord is gracious: unto whom coming a living stone, rejected indeed of men, but with God elect, precious, ye also, as living stones, are built up a spiritual house, to be a holy priesthood, to offer up spiritual sacrifices, acceptable to God through Jesus Christ."

It is our Holy Priesthood to offer up spiritual sacrifices acceptable to the Father through Jesus Christ.

That is our daily worship, our daily fellowship with Him.

We always come to our Father in the Name of His Beloved Son.

We come with thanksgiving; we come with worship; we come with love.

We bring the fruit of lips.

Would that our hearts could understand what this means.

Our words are the fruit of the vine. "I am the vine, and ye are the branches," Jesus said.

And here is lip fruit: our words from which the wine of life can be made.

How it does touch our hearts to think that He drinks of the fruit of our lips.

Jesus said, "I am that living water." Now we can understand that.

Heb. 13:15 makes us know as we never did, the holy privilege of speech. "Through Him let us offer up a sacrifice of praise to God continually, that is, the fruit of lips which make confession to His name."

Now we can understand what it means to come into His Presence.

You come with your petitions.

You come with your heartaches.

You come with your burden, and He partakes of the fruit of your lips.

Oh, how priceless are your words to Him!

The rent veil, the tender heart invitation to come boldly to the Throne of Grace, all mean something to us now.

We are coming in through the Living Way that Jesus opened by His great sacrifice; by His victory over the Adversary, that made our New Birth possible and our standing as sons a reality.

Ours is a two-fold Priesthood. We are not only a Holy Priesthood, but we are a Royal Priesthood.

This is pictured in 1 Pet. 2:9-10: "But ye are an elect race, a royal priesthood, a holy nation, a people for God's own possession, that ye may show forth the excellencies of him who called you out of darkness into his marvelous light: who in time past were no people, but now are the people of God: who had not obtained mercy, but now have obtained mercy."

This is our public ministry.

Whether it be as a layman or a preacher, we are showing forth in our daily walk, in our conversation, the fruits of this Royal Priesthood.

You see, we belong to the Throne.

We belong to Royalty, and we are showing forth His Excellencies.

We are advertising His love, His grace, His longsuffering.

We are advertising Eternal Life, His very Nature.

We belong to Royalty.

Is it any wonder that we have access to the Throne?

Is it any wonder that we can come boldly to the Throne of Grace?

We are walking up the New and Living Way!

Prayer should be as natural as breathing and as enjoyable as eating.

Prayer should be as unconscious as our communication with each other.

It should not be the child of need, but should be based on a spiritual fellowship with the Father and with the Master so that our needs are His needs; for we are not our own, we are a part of Him.

Our body is not our own.

The property we control is not our own.

Our abilities are not our own.

They are all His.

So we are laboring together with Him, and what we have considered personal needs are really His needs.

The work that we are doing is His work, so that prayer is not what we have thought it was; but it is a fellowship, a sharing; it is community interest.

We are one in this, just as the vine and the branch are one. The branch cannot bear fruit alone, and the vine cannot bear fruit without the branch.

So prayer is simply talking it over with Him, getting His views, His will, His plans, and our carrying out those plans with His grace, ability and wisdom.

Habits are children of our choice.

We are what we make ourselves.

This prayer habit will be born of your own will.

This habit is hard to form for most people. It should never be a duty, for just as we do not enjoy those who visit us because it is their duty, so it is with the Father.

We want those who love us to come because they cannot help it.

Prayer is a visit with our Father.

We should think of it as a rare opportunity.

Chapter The Second

THE PRAYER HABIT

THE names that are familiar to us in God's Westminster Abbey of the Church are the names of those who pray; men and women who have climbed the mountains of usefulness in the struggle with circumstances through prayer.

There is no denying that the lack of prayer is the bane of the individual member of the body of Christ.

Jesus was a man of prayer.

He taught prayer, not as a slavish duty, but as a glorious privilege.

I used to wonder why He needed to pray.

He took His human place, and lived the human life.

I have a conviction that He didn't draw upon the secret resources that belonged to Him, more than it is possible for us who live and walk in His Name.

Jesus' ministry in healing illustrated what our prayer life may do for us.

He didn't exercise His divine prerogatives during His three years' ministry any more than any child of God may exercise them.

He had a human body.

He had the limitations that go with the Incarnation.

The believer is a New Creation, created in Christ Jesus. He is brought into the family of God. He is an heir of God and a joint-heir with Jesus Christ.

He is a child of God.

The Spirit that raised Jesus from the dead dwells in his body. Plus this, Jesus has given him the power of attorney to use His Name.

The more that I study the life of Jesus, I am convinced that He did not exercise divine power in excess of what every intelligent child of God possesses today.

The difference is that Jesus knew what belonged to Him and Jesus used His rights.

We do not know what belongs to us. Not knowing what is ours, we cannot use our rights.

When Jesus cast out demons, He used authority that He has delegated to the the church.

He said, "In my Name ye shall cast out demons."

21

The forces of hell could not touch Him or injure Him; He was simply using the divine ability that is delegated to us.

"Ye shall take up serpents and they shall not injure you."

The poison of vipers has no power over the Christian's body, who knows his place in Christ.

The apostle Paul loosened the deadly fangs of a viper that had fastened itself into his hand, and shook the thing off without injury.

Paul simply illustrated what Jesus had promised.

Let me state it again: I am convinced that intelligent children of the Lord could walk in the same life and power and divine liberty as Jesus walked, if they understood their privileges.

He said, "If ye shall drink any deadly thing it shall not harm you."

Poison could not be administered to the Lord Jesus and take effect.

It cannot be administered to the body of Christ and take effect if the members of that body walk in the knowledge and liberty of the sons of God.

This is not extreme .

It is simply walking in the realm of Life.

We have been translated out of the realm of darkness; that is, the kingdom of weakness, darkness and ignorance.

We have been translated into the kingdom of the Son of His Love, which is the realm of wealth, of life, of light, joy, of peace, and of faith.

Let me state it again: Jesus in His earth walk, as the Incarnate Son of God, beginning with His baptism, lived exactly as every child of God should live today.

God wasn't any more His Father than He is ours.

He said, "The Father loveth you even as He loves me."

He was the Son of God.

You are a son of God.

He was Deity.

You are a partaker of the Divine Nature, that is Deity.

He had the Holy Spirit dwelling in Him.

You have the Holy Spirit dwelling in you.

The difference is that Jesus gave the Holy Spirit right of way in a sense of which we have never yet learned.

He took advantage of the God-life within Him in a way that we have never yet been able to take advantage of the God-life within us.

But, you say, Jesus was not mortal as we are.

That is true.

But, by faith the body is dead because of sin, but the spirit is life because of righteousness.

Our bodies shall not have dominion over us as we walk in the realm of God.

Again, Paul says that our bodies are dead, have lost their mortal effectiveness in reigning over our spirits.

I believe that God planned that we should walk in the fulness of the Divine Life; that we should dare to take our positions as sons and daughters of God; and that the hour is coming before the Lord's return in which a remnant of the body will rise and walk before God the Father in the fulness of the New Creation Life.

Disease will not be able to lay hold upon us.

Ignorance and fear will be banished, because the Wisdom that comes from above that is in Jesus, will lead us into the full dream, ambitions and purposes of our Father.

Now, I want you to notice that God has made Jesus to be our Redemption.

Paul said, in Eph. 1:7: "In whom we have our Redemption."

1 Cor. 1:30 declares that He "is our Redemption."

You dare to measure that!

You dare to set limits on that!

The limits of that Redemption are the limits of Jesus.

He was made unto us Wisdom from God.

The limits of that Wisdom are the limits of the Eternal Son of God.

He is made unto us Sanctification.

The limits of that Sanctification are the limits of Jesus.

He is our Life, and the limits of that Life are the limits of the Life of the Son of God.

You see, our feeble reasoning has pushed faith out of the arena. The Devil can combat successfully against our reason.

But if Faith gets reason's place, Satan is whipped.

The great body of the most advanced Bible teachers today, are held in the bondage of Sense Knowledge.

Their interpretations are often evasions.

Because of the opinions of men, they dare not take their real place.

Consequently, the Word of God has little effect.

Let us humbly and fearlessly, and in the Name of the Lord Jesus Christ, take our place.

If we are New Creations created in Christ Jesus, let us ask the Father to set the limits of that New Creation, instead of allowing theologians to do it.

Faith will lead you where reason cannot walk.

Reason has never been a mountain climber.

Faith, like a mountain sheep, can scale the loftiest mountain peaks without fear.

I offer this as a subject for meditation, not controversy.

I offer this as a contribution after years of heart-searching, of out-reaching after the bigger, fuller life in Christ.

I know it is not in the Realm of Reason, but I know it is where Faith walks; and God is challenging us in these last days to get the light and the knowledge that will fit us for the closing of this dispensation.

The message that John Wesley brought was truth, but it was only part of the truth.

Calvin had only a little of the light.

There have been revelations continually from the Word during these hundreds of years.

Don't you think it is time that we passed out of the swaddling clothes period into the stature of the perfect man in Christ Jesus?

So, let us dare to climb the heights of God.

Let us say without fear, "I am what He says I am."

"He is in me what He says He is."

"I can do, with His ability in me, what He says I can."

This makes life big and rich.

This makes us worthwhile to Him!

This will make us partners with Him.

We will be in that prized inner-circle with Him, one of the trusted ones.

When He has a difficult mission, He will call on us.

You see, He will find it easy to reach us as we constantly visit Him.

Take your place!

Enjoy your rights!

All Kinds of Prayer

Eph. 6:10 (Moffatt): "Hold your ground, tighten the shield of truth about you, wear integrity as your coat of mail, have your feet shod with the stability of the gospel of peace, above all, take faith as your shield to enable you to quench the fire-tipped darts flung by the evil one. Put on salvation as your helmet, take the Spirit as your sword, (That is, the Word of God), praying at all times in the spirit, with all manner of prayer and entreaty . . . be alive to that, attend to it unceasingly."

You will notice by this translation that the object of the Christian soldier's coat of mail or armor, is that he may enter the prayer fight.

Preaching and personal work are God-honored and blessed vocations or ministries, but prayer is the foundation of it all.

A man might preach with the eloquence of a Beecher and be the most skilled of diplomats as a soul winner, but he will fall short of his ministry in both fields if he isn't backed up by the prayer life.

The failure of all Christian enterprises is a prayer failure.

Prayer alone gives success.

There are many different kinds of prayer.

There is simple petition lifting its sentences in Jesus' Name to the heart of Love.

There is persistent, tenacious prayer that will not yield until the answer comes.

There is prevailing prayer that overcomes every obstacle, that finally lands the answer in the harbor of peace.

There is battle prayer, with its tears and agony, its intense yearning.

There is the quiet prayer of faith whose voice is never lifted above a whisper, but whose persistent faith shakes the very throne of heaven.

There is prayer without ceasing that seems to perfume every act of the persistent pray-er.

Then, there is the unconscious prayer attitude.

Paul says by the Spirit: "Praying with all kinds of prayer."

How desperately the nation needs it.

How desperately the church needs it.

Nothing can take the place of prayer.

Every believer should go into the school of prayer with Christ and actually learn the secret of prayer, the precious ministry of intercession.

The prayer of Intercession is the prayer for another, not for self. It is the prayer that passes out from your domain, your realm, into the realm of another.

Jesus ever lives to make Intercession at the right hand of the Father.

The Holy Spirit in us oft-times makes Intercession that cannot be uttered in words.

Oft-times we are depressed; we cannot understand it or see any reason for it; it is the Holy Spirit in agony reaching through us to the Father.

If our spirits were only fruitful, perhaps we could understand the language and the agony of the Spirit in His mighty outreaching toward the throne of grace.

If our lives were only more perfectly under His sway, He might be able to breathe His passion through our conscious faculties, in His mighty agony for lost men and women.

Oft-times our spirits are dull, and He cannot communicate His passion and yearning through them to our minds.

So, it becomes unintelligible agony, "groanings that cannot be uttered."

I suppose this is the reason why certain men and women are led to become the prayer channels for a whole congregation.

So few of us, in our busy lives, take time to pray, that the Spirit searches through the congregation for the willing hearts that will deny themselves some of the common pleasures and will be first in the line of prayer instead of last.

On these willing hearts rolls the burden of the entire church.

Thank God, that in our church are found those who are willing to set aside whole nights of prayer; who will leave the joy of visiting with loved ones, and hide away alone with Him to take my burden and yours that we have in some way failed to roll on the Lord.

They encompass our Jericho with their persistent intercession.

It is a pity that more of us do not force ourselves into a life of prayer.

We have the time.

We use it in useless talk, or careless reading.

While the Spirit is searching for an outlet He must pass us by because we are not ready.

Oh, I beseech you, Reader, not to talk about it any more, or plan when you will do it, but begin it now.

Force yourself into the prayer life. Regardless of how you feel, drive yourself to prayer.

You will be amazed how halting and stumbling will be your first attempts.

You have been rated, perhaps, as an unusual Christian worker in the Church.

Men look upon you as an outstanding Christian, but if they knew that in behind your public profession there was an empty closet, or an unused prayer room, they would be amazed.

If you live with the Lord in secret, you will be able to pray with great freedom in public.

Unconsciously we call upon the people to pray who are on praying terms with the Lord.

Seldom will a spiritual mind reach out to an unspiritual life for help.

It is only when we are clutching at straws that we do it.

You see, prayer has several elements.

It brings you into personal fellowship and touch with the Father, and with the Holy Spirit, and with Jesus.

All three of the Godhead are brought into the prayer life.

You are praying to the Father.

You are praying in the Name of Jesus.

You are praying through the Holy Spirit.

Your prayer is based upon the Word.

It brings this earth heart of ours into contact with the heavenly center of all divine power and activity.

You can't spend any length of time in prayer without being affected by it.

The quietness, the unshaken faith, the deep, unsounded peace that pervades the Godhead, will overflow into the pray-er's life.

Said an anxious and nervous mòther: "You will have to forgive me, children, but I forgot to visit the Master this morning, and so I lack His quietness and His strength."

Many of us can make that confession, that our irritability, weakness, and lack of spiritual insight comes from not sitting in the presence of the Master.

One cannot spend an hour in conscious communion with the Father, the Son, the Spirit and the Word without carrying away from that trysting place the fragrance that fills the atmosphere.

There is a heavenly fragrance about Jesus that lingers with the pray-ers.

They are slow to speak.

They are slow to judge.

They are quick to love and quick to help.

There is a holy calmness about their lives that challenges the restless ones; they crave that quietness of spirit.

Again, we cannot spend time with them without partaking of their stability and their unshakableness.

One who is easily disturbed, and who in the jolts of life is unseated, will find a new strength and steadiness that will make him a blessing to the world, by spending just a little time with the Rock of our Strength.

You see, a few moments with Him tunes us up, fills the battery, adjusts the carburetor, and makes it easy for us to face life's uneven conditions.

It gives us poise and holy dignity in our contacts.

Faith makes us an intelligent victor.

Faith makes mountains and difficulties take their true position.

You can't sit with the God of all Faith and all Love, for one half hour each day, without unconsciously breathing in the Faith of God.

What would it mean to you, if Jesus should come into your home as He came into the home of Mary and Martha?

You would take time to visit with Him!

"Jesus answered and said unto him, If a man love me, he will keep my word: and my Father will love him, and we will come unto him, and make our abode with him." (John 14:23)

You love Him, invite Him into your home, and then get acquainted with Him.

Learn to talk things over with Him.

He is there; visit with Him!

Remember, He loves you, is interested in all your problems.

He will make His Word answer every question; He will make Himself real in your life and home.

Prayer On a Winning Basis

He made prayer a winning business proposition.

We didn't ask Him to do it.

We didn't send our representative and say, "Now, Father, we want you to give us certain promises and certain abilities."

No. He did it all. He planned it all for us.

He based a prayer life upon His own Word.

It was a daring thing for Him to do, but He believed that we would believe.

He dared to give His Son.

He dared to give man Eternal Life.

He dared to make us New Creations.

Why? Because He believed that man would respond to His love and that man, when challenged by such grace, would meet it with a glad response.

And so we are fellowshipping Him in His faith fight for a lost race.

We are helping the men for whom His Son died and has redeemed.

Our combat is warring against God's enemy.

It is saving the men for whom Christ died.

It is making strong the weak.

It is giving God's children a chance for winning in life's fight.

We are the instruments. We are the forerunners. We are the pioneers in this marvelous life of faith.

We are joining the men of all the ages who have dared to walk where paths have never been.

We are opening channels for His grace to reach the human race.

We are God's under-engineers. We are building roads for others to walk upon.

Our faith life has joined with God's faith life and we have

become His "tilled land," "His fellow-workers".

We are the branches that are bearing the real fruit from the real vine.

We are opening channels through which He can pour Himself out on man.

Our ministry is not a failure. We are winning.

We are making out of these failure-men, successes.

Our union with Him is beckoning other men to dare come into the union too.

They see failures transfigured into successes.

They see men who have been held for years absolute slaves to narcotics and drink, set free to walk in the fulness of their liberty in Christ.

And those in bondage reach their hands out for help, and our Father grasps them and lifts them up onto the solid rock.

Come on you pray-ers, join this mighty group of intercessors who are making the desert places blossom like the rose.

Come on you men and women who have never made prayer a business. Make your investment of time. Learn the art, yes, the secret of this the greatest business of the age.

Throw yourself open. Let Him pour Himself through you until your home and your business and your associates will feel the throb of His mighty life and the lift of His love.

Let me state it with all the simplicity possible, that you can't have prayers answered without having Miracles performed.

Prayer and Miracles

If you deny that Miracles are for this age, you deny the need, and the privileges and the benefits of prayer.

The two-fold value of prayer lies first in sitting in His presence, or in direct Fellowship with the Father.

The second benefit is the answer that comes to us.

John says, "If we ask anything according to His will, we know that He heareth us, and if we know that He hears us, we know that we have the petitions which we have asked."

For God the Father to hear my prayer is equivalent to His answering it.

Now, for God to hear me is a Miracle.

For God to answer my prayer, regardless of its nature, is a Miracle.

Whether my petition is for a postage stamp or for a million dollars, it is a miracle.

Any divine intervention, any arrest of the laws of nature that comes in answer to Faith, is a Miracle.

If prayer brings an answer, that answer is a Miracle. It is then that Faith has its true place.

The instant that you say there are no Miracles in this dispensation, you deny that our walk is a walk by Faith, and you declare that our walk is a walk by Reason.

I challenge you to find one place where God tells us as believers to walk by Reason.

God is a Faith God.

We are a Faith Family.

We are all born by Faith.

We live by Faith.

By Faith we live, breathe, and have our being in Christ.

If there are no Miracles, then there is no reason for Faith.

If there are no Miracles, God can't answer prayer, because He can't answer prayer of any character that is not a Miracle.

You men and women who tell me that you believe the Bible to be the Word of God, that it is God-breathed and without error in the original, and then, in the same breath, tell me that the Day of Miracles is past, you are the most illogical thinkers, the most inconsistent believers that the Devil ever deluded.

I believe profoundly that the Devil is the deceiver of the whole inhabited earth and of that type of Christian in particular.

So, let us reverently come back to God.

Let us take our place.

If we pray at all, we expect prayer to be answered.

If that prayer is answered, God has done it; and if God has answered prayer He has performed something outside of the Realm of Reason.

We will have to give up our prayer life utterly, or we will have to believe in Miracles.

I believe in Miracles.

I believe in divine intervention.

I believe that the prayer of Faith reaches God our Father, and when it reaches Him He acts in response to that Faith.

When He acts in response to our Faith, His action is above our reason. It is in the Realm of Miracles.

For me to deny the privilege and benefits of prayer would raise a storm of protest among those who deny Miracles today.

I want you to see, my brother, as you read this today, that your position is untenable.

Faith causes a man to act like God.

Love makes him like God.

The Supernatural

Prayer is an excursion into the supernatural realm.

You are in the Throne Room in the Presence of God, of All Ability. He has promised to hear your petition and to give you your request. You have come on the ground of His Word.

He said: "Whatsoever ye shall ask of the Father in my Name he will give it you."

You understand that the words that Jesus spoke were His Father's words; so you come now with the Father's words in your lips, and you are making your appeal on the ground of His own Word.

Taking a Son's Place

You are not a servant.

You are not a slave.

You are a son. You are taking Jesus' place, acting in His stead, doing the Father's will.

You may know that you are the Father's will just as Jesus was the Father's will, because of His own will He begat you.

You are the fruit of His own Word. You came into being by His own power and ability. You have received Eternal Life, His very Nature.

You recognize your place in Christ. You are acting the part of a Son.

The great unsaved world must know what He has done for them in Christ; and so you are taking His ability, doing your part in the saving of men as Jesus did His part.

You belong to a supernatural order of being whether you recognize it or not, whether you have taken your place or not. You have the ability of the indwelling presence.

You have the wisdom that Jesus had in His earth walk because Jesus has been made unto you wisdom.

You can think of yourself as linked up with Ability, linked with Omnipotence.

You remember He said: "And nothing shall be impossible to you."

I know that Sense Knowledge reasoning shrinks from this, but here is where the challenge of grace leads you.

We dare to take our place, dare confess what we are, dare confess that He made us what we are, that we can do what He says we can do because He is at work within us.

We have His Word that He is in us. The latent ability and energy within us is His Who gave it to us.

This makes the prayer life a master thing.

You are not asking for the possible. You are always praying for the impossible. You are asking for things that can't be done by any human method.

Fasting and long hours of prayer do not build faith.

Reading books about faith, and about men of faith and their exploits stirs in the heart a deep passion for faith, but does not build faith.

The Word alone is the source of faith.

But the Word will not build faith unless it becomes a part of us. "If ye abide in me and my words have their place in you." That is, they have their place in our conduct.

Jesus gave us the key. He said, "The words that I speak are not mine, but my Father's."

And the works that He did were not His, but His Father's.

Jesus acted on His Father's words.

Jesus never needed faith. He had it unconsciously.

Faith is built in us by the Word being built into us, by our acting upon it.

It is "the Word of faith," and so as the Father builds that into us in our daily walk, faith becomes an unconscious asset.

We come to realize that we are a part of Him as a branch is a part of the vine; that He is a part of us as the vine is a part of the branch; that we have His life, we have His ability, we have His love nature, we have His strength.

That gives us an unconscious certainty as we go into His presence.

We know that we are working together with Him to one common end.

We know that He is the strength of our life.

We know that He is our ability.

We know that we are His righteousness in Christ.

We know that He needs us to carry out His will, and so we are taking our place as a son carrying out His dream for man.

Chapter The Third

HOW FAITH IS BUILT

HERE cannot be a real prayer life that is not built upon the Word. The Word is the source of all Faith.

The faith must be a quiet assurance, an unconscious faith, something that you do not even think about.

You can't conceive of Jesus saying to himself: "If I only had faith."

Men and women who have really wrought mighty things have been those who never thought about their faith life.

The Word was a reality.

What He said solved the problem.

This Word is revelation knowledge.

It is God deigning to speak with man.

The Reality of the Incarnation

First there must be a reality of the Incarnation.

John 1:14: "And the Word became flesh, and dwelt among us, (and we beheld his glory, glory as of the only begotten from the Father), full of grace and truth."

The Incarnation cannot be a doctrine or a theory or a metaphysical concept.

It must be as real as your birth is to you.

Not something to argue about, but an absolute fact that God has broken into the human realm and has given to the senses a testimony of His reality.

I can never forget when I knew actually that God had been and was manifest in the flesh.

I had an unconscious background of doubt; that disappeared, and another background of absolute certainty took its place.

Reality of His Resurection

Many of us have revelled in His earth walk, following Him step by step in His miraculous career.

We were thrilled at the demonstrations of Divine ability that characterized Him in every crisis.

He faced a dead Lazarus as simply as you and I would face any ordinary event in life.

He was perfectly quiet in the midst of the storm on the Sea of Galilee.

He walked on the waves that night amid the tumult of a raging storm as quietly as you walk up and down on the sidewalk in front of your home.

There was a royalty about His faith; a divine dignity that thrills us.

But was He raised from the dead?

He raised others. Was He raised?

I fought this for years. It was an unknown battle to those about me.

I used to say, "If He was actually raised from the dead, then His deity and His substitutionary work are realities."

One day as I was reading John 20:1-10 I saw the miracle.

The problem of the Resurrection of Jesus centers first around the question: "Was He dead?" or as one skeptic declares, "He had swooned."

John 19:30-34: "When Jesus therefore had received the vinegar, he said, It is finished: and he bowed his head, and gave up his spirit.

"The Jews therefore, because it was the Preparation, that the bodies should not remain on the cross upon the sabbath (for the day of that sabbath was a high day), asked of Pilate that their legs might be broken, and that they might be taken away. The soldiers therefore came, and brake the legs of the first, and of the other that was crucified with him: but when they came to Jesus, and saw that he was dead already, they brake not his legs: howbeit one of the soldiers with a spear pierced his side, and straightway there came out blood and water."

That Roman spearhead was four or five inches wide, and when he stood there underneath the Master and thrust the spear up into the side of Jesus, it must have penetrated the sack that holds the heart.

What had happened?

Jesus had died!

The body had grown cold.

His heart had been ruptured when He uttered that cry, "It is finished."

And out through the rupture in the heart flowed the blood into the sack until it was filled.

The body rapidly grows cold. As it does, the blood separates. The white serum settles to the bottom, and the red corpuscles rise to the top; and as the body grows colder, the red corpuscles coagulate.

When the spear pierced the sack that held the blood, the white serum or water flowed out. Then the red corpuscles slowly oozed out and rolled down the side of His body onto the ground.

Jesus was dead.

As soon as the Master was dead, loving hearts began to prepare for His burial.

John 19:38: "And after these things Joseph of Arimathea, being a disciple of Jesus, but secretly for fear of the Jews, asked of Pilate that he might take away the body of Jesus: and Pilate gave him leave. He came therefore, and took away his body."

You understand that in every family among the wealthy Jews, there was a slave who understood embalming, for that class always embalmed their loved ones.

John 19:39-40: "And there came also Nicodemus, he who at the first came to him by night, bringing a mixture of myrrh and aloes, about a hundred pounds. So they took the body of Jesus, and bound it in linen cloths with the spices, as the custom of the Jews is to bury."

The body was first washed, and then the cloth was torn up into narrow strips and smeared with the sticky substance. Each finger and toe and hand and foot was wrapped with these strips until the legs and arms and body were completely encased in this sticky substance. The head and neck were completely covered except the face.

When it was finished, over the chest and torso there was an inch to an inch and a half of this cloth covered with that sticky substance.

The body was then put into Joseph's tomb.

The climate was about the same as they have in Southern California. In a few hours the embalming garment would become a solid mass, and Jesus' body would be completely imprisoned in the grave clothes.

If He were not dead, this would cause Him to die.

The face was yet to be embalmed. Loved ones laid a napkin upon His face, heavily saturated with something to preserve the face until the third day when loving hands would finish the embalming.

Jesus was dead.

The Roman government had pronounced Him dead.

The soldiers had pronounced Him dead.

The Jews knew He was dead.

John 20:1-10: "Now on the first day of the week cometh Mary Magdalene early, while it was yet dark, unto the tomb, and seeth the stone taken away from the tomb. She runneth therefore, and cometh to Simon Peter, and to the other disciple whom Jesus loved, and saith unto them, They have taken away the Lord out of the tomb, and we know not where they have laid him.   Peter therefore went forth, and the other disciple, and they went toward the tomb.   And they ran both together: and the other disciple outran Peter, and came first to the tomb; and stooping and looking in, he seeth the linen cloths lying: yet entered he not in.   Simon Peter therefore also cometh, following him, and entered into the tomb: and he beholdeth the linen cloths lying, and the napkin, that was upon his head, not lying with the linen cloths, but rolled up in a place by itself. Then entered in therefore the other disciple also, who came first to the tomb, and he saw and believed.   For as yet they knew not the scripture, that he must rise again from the dead.   So the disciples went away again unto their own home."

You notice carefully the ninth and tenth verses. They knew not that Jesus must arise again from the dead. None of them believed in His resurrection so you can understand their surprise when Mary came to the house where Peter and John were stopping, and cried, "They have taken away the Lord out of the tomb, and we know not where they have laid him."

Nothing was more sacred to the Jews than the dead. Mary had been filled with anger and sorrow that someone had dared to desecrate the tomb.

Peter and John ran together. John is younger, lighter of foot. He outruns his heavier partner and arrives at the tomb first. It was a sepulchre cut out of a solid ledge. John stops and reverently looks into the darkened tomb. Peter comes, just bows his head, and enters the tomb. John follows. The grave clothes are lying there on the floor. He sees the napkin that was upon Jesus' face folded up and lying on a niche in the tomb.

John 20:8 says: "Then entered in therefore the other disciple also, who came first to the tomb, and he saw, and believed."

What did John see?

He saw the empty cocoon lying there upon the floor. It had become so hard and stiff that it would almost support one's knee as you pressed upon it. But it was empty.

The body of Jesus had come out of that little narrow aperture at the face.

If John had seen that someone with a knife had ripped that cocoon open and taken the body of Jesus, he would never have believed; the empty cocoon convinced John that Jesus was risen from the dead.

In my imagination I had been with Peter and John when Mary came with her anger and distress, crying, "They have taken away the body."

I had gone with them to the tomb. I had stood there in my imagination looking into the tomb.

I entered into the tomb with John, and I saw what John saw; and for the first time in my life I knew that Jesus Christ had risen from the dead.

It has never been a theological dogma since that hour.

Jesus was raised from the dead.

But what does that Resurrection mean?

That the sin problem was settled.

That Satan was conquered.

Humanity was redeemed.

That God can now on legal grounds impart His Nature, Eternal Life, to man and make him a New Creation.

At last man can become God's actual child, a very son.

There can be perfect fellowship between them.

When God imparted His Nature to man, He imparted His Righteousness. So man is a partaker of the Divine 'Nature and the Righteousness of God.

Man can stand in the Father's presence as did Jesus in His earth walk.

Now God can give the Holy Spirit to live permanently in the body of this New Creation, and He can build into that New Creation through the Word, the very character and nature of the Incarnate One; so that we can say softly: "It is no longer I that live, but Christ liveth in me."

Now I know that Rom. 4:25 is a reality: "Who was delivered up on the account of my trespasses and raised because I was justified." (Lit. Trans.)

Reality of His Redemption

The Church has had a theological conception of our Redemption. It has never been a part of our daily walk.

Col. 1:13-14: "Who delivered us out of the authority of darkness and translated us into the kingdom of the Son of his love, in whom we have our Redemption."

And Eph. 1:7 says that that Redemption is according to the riches of His grace.

In the mind of the Father that Redemption is a reality.

It would have been a total failure otherwise.

That Redemption meant that Satan had been utterly defeated, stripped of his authority and dominion so that any man no matter what his condition has been, how deeply he has been enmeshed in sin, can by whispering the name of Jesus and by confessing His

Lordship, step out of bondage into perfect liberty.

Rom. 6:14: "For sin shall not have dominion over you," or "Satan shall not lord it over you."

It has made the new man, the New Creation, a master of sin.

In the name of Jesus the weakest child of God is an absolute master of Satan and demons.

That Redemption is a reality.

You who have received Eternal Life, as you read this, can whisper, "I am free. The Son has made me free, and I am free in reality." (John 8:36. Most of these verses are a literal translation or copied from some of our modern translations.)

That Redemption is a reality to the man who knows his place in Christ.

You cannot be in Christ and not be free from the dominion of the Devil.

Reality of the New Creation

What substitutions we have had for the New Creation.

We have called it "Forgiveness of Sins," "Being Converted," "Getting Religion," "Joining the Church," and many others.

It is just one thing: A New Creation, a child of God, a partaker of the Divine Nature. These all represent the one fact that you have passed out of death, Satanic Nature, into Life, the realm of God.

That is not just forgiveness of sins, but it is the impartation of a New Nature.

The old self, the old man was crucified with Christ.

A new man was resurrected and when you accepted Jesus Christ as Savior and confessed Him as Lord, God imparted His own Nature, Eternal Life to you and you became "a new species," a new man over which Satan has no dominion.

Reality in Jesus' Name

How little we have appreciated this. It is one of the greatest gifts the Church has ever had given her.

Before Jesus left us He gave to the Church a legal right to the use of His Name. John 15:16: "Whatsoever ye shall ask of the Father in my name, he will give it you."

John 16:23-24 (Note this translation): "And in that day ye shall not pray to me. Verily, verily, I say unto you, if ye shall ask anything of the Father he will give it you in my name. Hitherto have ye asked nothing in my name. Ask and ye shall receive that your joy may be made full."

Here He gives us the power of attorney to go to the Father and make our requests.

When you pray in that Name, it is as though Jesus prayed.

There can be no denial.

You remember Jesus said at the tomb of Lazarus: "I thank thee, Father, that thou dost always hear me." That is the ground for your assurance.

John 14:13-14 He gives us the use of the Name: "And whatsoever ye shall ask or demand in my name, that will I do, that the Father may be glorified in the Son. If ye shall ask anything in my name, that will I do."

This is not prayer. This is described in Acts 3:6 where Peter and John heal a man at the Beautiful Gate by saying, "In the name of Jesus Christ of Nazareth, rise and walk."

It is as Paul used it in Acts 16:18 where he spoke to the demon in the girl and said, "In the name of Jesus come out of her."

Or as the Name was used on the day of Pentecost when they baptized those people in the Name of Jesus.

When we pray we say, "Our Father, in Jesus Name."

That is our approach.

That gives us the assurance of a hearing.

Jesus said, recorded in John 14:17 speaking of the Holy Spirit, "He is with you, but he shall be in you."

Reality of Indwelling

On the day of Pentecost we see four things take place in that upper room.

"Suddenly there came from heaven the sound of a rushing of a mighty wind and it filled all the room where they were sitting." The disciples were immersed in the Holy Spirit.

And when they were immersed, they received Eternal Life, were made New Creations.

They were the first people aside from Jesus that were ever born again. Jesus, you know, is the "first born." (Col. 1:-8 and Rev. 1:5)

The second thing that happened, tongues of fire sat upon the brow of each one, indicating the method of propagating this Gospel of the grace of God. It is going to be with tongues of fire.

For example, Steven's tongue couldn't be withstood, so they had to kill him to get rid of his tongue of fire.

And the third thing, they were all filled with the Holy Spirit. He couldn't come in until they were recreated.

And the fourth, they all spake with other tongues.

But note that the great thing was they had not only received Eternal Life, but they had the One who had raised Jesus from the dead now living in them.

We have made a great deal of receiving the Holy Spirit.

It has been majored and we have ignored the fact of His being in us.

1 John 4:4: "Ye are of God my little children, and have overcome them because greater is He that is in you, than he that is in the world."

Phil. 2:13: "For it is God who is at work within you, willing and working his own good pleasure."

Not only are we Born Again, have become the very sons and daughters of God, but He comes and makes His home in us.

Reality of Righteousness

The ministry has kept the Church in the bondage of sin-consciousness ever since the Reformation.

None of us have ever been able to get away from it.

Most of our hymns are about sin.

Most every sermon is about sin.

The Church has never known of her absolute freedom from sin-consciousness.

Heb. 10:1-14 should be studied very carefully. We haven't space to quote it all.

First it tells how the blood of bulls and goats couldn't take away sin, for if it could the worshippers having been once cleansed would have no more consciousness of sins. "But in those sacrifices there is a remembrance made of sins year by year."

That makes us think of the altar service where we ask the believer to keep coming Sunday after Sunday to be cleansed from sin.

The blood of Jesus Christ hasn't meant more to some of us than the blood of bulls and goats meant to the Jew.

For it was impossible that the blood of bulls and goats should take away sin.

The eleventh verse: "And every priest standeth day by day ministering and offering the same sacrifices which can never take away sin. But he, when he had offered one sacrifice for sins forever, sat down on the right hand of God; for by one offering he hath perfected forever them that are sanctified."

He dealt with the sin problem for us perfectly when we were recreated and received the nature and life of God.

At that time He not only put our sin away, but He remitted all that we had ever committed; and at the same time he imparted His own Nature, Righteousness, to us.

2 Cor. 5:21: "Him who knew no sin, God made to become sin that we might become the righteousness of God in Him," and by that New Creation we have become the Righteousness of God.

So Rom. 3:26 has become a reality: "That he, (God,) might himself be righteous and the righteousness of him who hath faith in Jesus." (Marg.)

Here God declares that He becomes the righteousness of the man who accepts His Son as a Savior.

1 Cor. 1:30 declares that Jesus has been made to be our righteousness.

God is our righteousness, Jesus is our righteousness, and by the New Creation we have become the righteousness of God in Him.

But you ask, "What is the righteousness of God?"

It is the ability to stand in the Father's presence without the sense of guilt, condemnation or inferiority.

It is the ability to stand there as the very sons and daughters of God Almighty so that you can go boldly unto the throne of grace and make your petitions just as Jesus would if He were here.

Some Faith Facts

Faith in the Father is not built upon the word of man but upon His own Word.

Man's testimony to the truth of the Word has its place, but it cannot take the place of the Word itself.

The Word is the Father speaking.

It is as though the Master were here now in person; that Word is taking His place.

That Word has given us life and made us new creations.

That Word has sustained us and upheld us.

It is the Word of faith that proceeds from the very heart of the Father of faith.

The Word is a part of the Father Himself.

I feed on it.

I breathe it into my spirit.

It is being built into my spirit-consciousness.

Its absolute integrity, its life-giving quality has impregnated my very being.

Man's word like grass, withers.

God's Word like Himself, can never die, can never lose its freshness, its power, its ability to recreate, to strengthen and give courage.

You see, the Word in the lips of faith becomes just like the Word in Jesus' lips.

The Word in lips of doubt and fear is a dead thing; but in the lips of faith, it becomes life-giving, dominant.

Through it the sick are healed; Satan's captives are set free.

This living Word in the lips of faith is God's answer to the heart cry of man.

Man's word may fascinate and satisfy reason for a time, but the heart demands the Word of God.

This Word illumined by the Holy Spirit is God's light on life's pathway.

The Word is a part of Himself.

You can lean on the Word as you would lean on Him.

You can rest in the Word as you would rest in Him.

You can act on the Word as you would act if He had just spoken to you.

The Word is always Now.

Our modern psychological religions are children of the senses; they use the Bible and quote from it, but it is only man's literature to them. Their writings can't feed the hungry spirit of man; they simply entertain and thrill the people of the senses.

These eternal spirits of ours crave the bread of God. Jesus is the bread of Life; they that feed on Him, have no appetite for the theories of men.

Don't waste time with the philosophies of men. There is no life in them.

In Him is Life, and that Life is our Light.

His word alone can answer the heart-cry of man.

Their words may answer the cry of lost reason-ruled souls groping in the sense realm for light, but never the cry of the heart.

Jesus' bold and continual confession is our example. We are what He made us to be.

Jesus confessed what He was. Sense knowledge could not understand it.

We are to confess what we are in Christ. Men of the senses will not understand us.

To confess that you are redeemed, that your Redemption is an actual reality, that you are delivered out of Satan's dominion and authority, would be a daring confession to make.

To confess that you are an actual New Creation created in Christ Jesus, that you are a partaker of the very nature and life of Deity, would amaze your friends.

It isn't confessing it once, but daily affirming your relationship to Him, confessing your Righteousness, your ability to stand in His presence without the sense of guilt or inferiority.

Dare to stand in the presence of sense knowledge facts, and declare that you are what God says you are!

For instance sense knowledge declares that I am sick with an incurable illness. I confess that God laid that disease on Jesus and that Satan has no right to put it on me; that, "by his stripes I am healed." I am to hold fast to my confession in the face of apparent sense knowledge contradiction.

Sense knowledge says that it is not true; that I am confessing an untruth. But I am confessing what God says.

You see, there are two kinds of Truth: sense knowledge Truth, and revelation Truth; and they are usually opposed to each other.

I live in the new realm above the senses, so I hold fast to my confession that I am what the Word says I am.

Suppose my senses have revealed the fact that I am in great need financially. The Word declares, "My God shall supply every need of yours."

I call His attention to what the senses have intimated, and He knows that my expectations are from Him. I refuse to be intimidated by sense evidences. I refuse to have my life governed by them. I know that greater is He that is in me than the forces that surround me.

The forces that oppose me are in the senses.

The power that is in me, is the Holy Spirit; and I know that spiritual forces are greater than the forces in the sense realm.

I maintain my confession of spiritual values, of spiritual realities in the face of sense contradictions.

Chapter The Fourth

THE TWO CONFESSIONS

AFTER having prayed for one the other morning, she was satisfied that she was perfectly healed, but now the symptoms have returned and her heart is disturbed. She wonders where the difficulty lies."

I asked this party, "Did you tell your husband when you met him at night that you were healed?"

"No, you see I wasn't sure yet. I didn't want to say anything until I was positive."

"But you had no pain? Was there any soreness?" I asked.

"Oh, that all left; but you see I have to be careful. My husband is skeptical and I didn't want to tell him I was healed until I was sure."

I can see where her difficulty lay. She did not believe the Word. Had she made her confession to her husband, the thing would never have come back. But she played into the hands of the Enemy, and he restored the same symptoms that she had had, and brought back the pain and soreness. This happened because she invited him to do it.

Had she dared to stand her ground on the Word, and hold fast to her confession that she was healed, he would have no ground of approach.

Our faith or unbelief is determined by our confession.

Few of us realize the effect of our spoken word on our own heart or on our Adversary.

He hears us make our confession of failure, of sickness, of lack, and apparently he doesn't forget; and we unconsciously go down to the level of our confession.

No one ever rises above it.

If you confess sickness, it develops sickness in your system.

If you confess doubt, the doubts become stronger.

If you confess lack of finances, it stops the money from coming in.

You say, "I can't understand this."

No. Because most of us live in the sense realm and spiritual things are very indistinct.

Heb. 4:14 must become a constant reality: "Having then a great high priest, who hath passed through the heavens, Jesus the Son of God, let us hold fast our confession."

Our confession is that the Word cannot be broken; that what the Father says is true.

When we doubt the Father, we are doubting His Word.

When we doubt His Word, it is because we believe something else that is contrary to that Word.

Our confidence may be in the arm of flesh; it may be in medicine; it may be in institutions; but whatever our confidence is in, if it contradicts the Word it destroys our faith life.

It destroys our prayers.

It brings us again into bondage.

Every person who walks by faith will have testings.

They do not come from the Father; they come from the Adversary.

He is refusing to allow you to escape him.

You become dangerous to the Adversary when you become strong enough to resist him—when you have learned to trust in the ability of the Father to meet your every need.

When that becomes a reality in your consciousness, the Adversary is defeated.

But as long as he can confuse the issue and keep you in a state of flux, you are at a disadvantage.

This book is written for one purpose: to strengthen your confidence in the Word; to make you know "that no Word from God is void of power" or can go by default.

There isn't power in all the universe to void one statement of fact in this Word.

He said, "I watch over my Word to perform it."

And again, "Whosoever believeth on him, shall not be put to shame."

Your confidence is in that unbroken, living Word, and you hold fast to your confession in the face of every assault of the enemy.

Note Conybeare's translation of Phil. 1:28: "And nowise terrified by its enemies; for their enmity is to them an evidence of perdition, but to you of salvation, and that from God."

Here is Moffat's translation: "Never be scared for a second by your opponents; your fearlessness is a clear omen of ruin for them and of your own salvation—at the hands of God."

2 Cor. 2:14-15 Moffat Trans.: "Wherever I go, I thank God, he makes my life a constant pageant of triumph in Christ, diffusing the perfume of his knowledge everywhere by me. I live for God

as the fragrance of Christ breathed alike by those who are being saved and by those who are perishing."

You take your position in Christ that you are more than a conqueror, that no matter what the testing may be God cannot let you fail.

You are not standing on sense evidence.

You are not standing on the faith of other people.

You are standing squarely upon His own Word.

Your confidence is not in the prayers of others, but in this unchanging, unbreakable Word; and you refuse to allow your lips to destroy the effectiveness of that Word in your case.

You hold fast to your confession though it would appear as though the prayer was never answered.

It is your quiet assurance in His Word that gives you the supremacy over your Adversaries.

You know that all authority is in the Name of Jesus; that every demon and every disease and every circumstance must bow to that Name.

Phil. 2:9-11: "Wherefore also God exalted him, and gave unto him the name which is above every name; that in the name of Jesus every knee should bow, of beings in heaven, beings on earth and that every tongue should confess that Jesus Christ is Lord, to the glory of God the Father."

You see that the Name of Jesus has all authority and you have a legal right to use that Name in every extremity.

You are His son, His own very child.

You have come to Him in the Name of Jesus for this need, and He is under obligation to see that you are not put to shame.

He is under obligation to make His Word good.

One said to me this morning, "God has tied Himself up by His Word. He cannot fail us. He cannot ignore us."

So let us hold fast to our confession and never cower for a moment no matter how sense knowledge may produce evidence to the contrary.

You are not standing on sense evidence.

Feelings and appearances have no place here.

This is God's field and God's alone.

Realization Follows Confessions

We walk in the light of our testimony—our faith never goes beyond our confession.

The Word becomes real only as we confess its reality. The reason for this is, "We walk by faith and not by sight."

Sense knowledge would confess only what it had seen, heard or felt.

The people who are seeking experiences always walk by the senses.

Our testimony of the reality of the Word is feared by Satan.

"That if thou shalt confess with thy mouth." This reacts on our heart just as doubt spoken by the lips reacts on our heart.

You talk of your doubts and your fears, and you destroy your faith.

You talk of the ability of the Father that is yours, and fill your lips with praise for answers to prayers that you have asked. Its reaction upon the heart is tremendous: Faith grows by leaps and bounds.

You talk about your trials and your difficulties, of your lack of faith, of your lack of money, and faith shrivels, loses its virility.

Your whole spirit life shrinks.

You study about what you are in Christ and then confess it boldly.

You dare to act on the Word in the face of sense knowledge opposition.

Regardless of appearance, you take your stand; make your confession and hold fast to it in the face of apparent impossibilities.

You see, faith doesn't ask for possible things. Faith is demanding the impossible.

Prayer is never for the possible, but always for the thing that is out of reason.

It is God who is at work with us, in us and for us.

"How shall he not with him freely give us all things."

You see, you are launching out into the realm of the impossible just as Abraham did when he asked for a son.

You're not asking for something you can do for yourself, but for something that is beyond reason.

Then you refuse to take counsel with fear or to entertain a doubt.

The hardest battles I have ever fought have been along this line.

The greatest battles I have ever won have been those that seemed the most impossible, where there was the greatest opposition, where reason discredited my faith.

I held fast to my confession and the Word was made good.

Confess your dominion over disease in Jesus' Name.

Never be frightened by any condition no matter how forbidding, how impossible the case may be.

It may be cancer, tuberculosis, or an accident in which death seems to be the master of the situation. You never give in.

You know you and God are masters of the situation.

You never for a moment lose your confession of your supremacy over the works of the Adversary.

This disease, this calamity is not of God. It has but one source, Satan.

And in Jesus' Name you are master. You have taken Jesus' place; you are acting in His stead.

You fearlessly take your position; confess your ability in Christ to meet any emergency.

Always remember that Jesus met defeat and conquered it. You are facing defeat everywhere as a master.

Don't let down. Keep your solid front.

Way's translation of Phil. 1:27-28: "Let your life as members of one communion be worthy of the glad tidings of the Messiah so that, whether I do come and see you, or whether I must still be afar and only hear news of you, I may know that you are standing firm, animated by one spirit; may know that with united soul you are working strenuously shoulder to shoulder for the faith of the glad tidings; may know that you are not cowed one whit by your adversaries. Their failure to daunt you is clear evidence—an actual sign from God—for them that their destruction is imminent; but for you, that salvation is yours."

That solid front spoken of in Col. 2:5 (Weymouth), "Yet in spirit I am present with you, and am delighted to witness your good discipline and the solid front presented by your faith in Christ," is the solid front presented to your enemy.

You can't be conquered.

Your spirit is whispering, "Nay, in all these things I am more than a conqueror."

Every disease is of the Adversary.

All kinds of sin are of the Adversary.

All opposition to the glad tidings is of the Adversary.

God and I are victors.

Greater is He that is in me than this opposition or this disease.

There is no need that is greater than my Lord.

There is no lack that He cannot meet.

This indomitable will that God has wrought in you cannot be overwhelmed, or conquered.

You remember what you are—you are a New Creation.

You are a branch of the vine.

You are an heir of God.

You are united with Him. You and He are one; and He is the greater part of that one.

There is no such thing as conquering God when His instrument refuses to admit that the enemy can overwhelm him.

You are that instrument.

"I have learned in whatsoever state I am in, therein to be independent of circumstances." Phil. 4:11 (Way Tran.)

Defeated With Your Own Lips

You said that you could not, and the moment that you said it you were whipped.

You said you did not have faith, and doubt arose like a giant and bound you.

You are imprisoned with your own words.

You talked failure and failure held you in bondage.

Prov. 6:2: "Thou art snared with the words of thy mouth. Thou art taken (captive) with the words of thy mouth."

Few of us realize that our words dominate us.

A young man said, "I was never whipped until I confessed I was whipped."

Another said, "The moment I began to make a bold, confident confession, a new courage that I had never known took possession of me."

Another young woman said, "My lips have been a constant curse. I have never been able to get the mastery of my lips."

A woman said the other day, "I always speak my mind." She has few friends. Only pity causes people to go see her. Her lips have been her curse.

It isn't so bad speaking your mind if you have the mind of Christ, but as long as you have a mind dominated by the devil, few people care to hear your mind.

Never talk failure.

Never talk defeat.

Never for a moment acknowledge that God's ability can't put you over.

Become "God-inside minded," remembering that greater is He that is in you than any force that can come against you; remembering that God created a universe with words; that words are more mighty than tanks or bombs, more mighty than the Army or Navy.

Learn to use words so they will work for you and be your servants.

Learn that your lips can make you a millionaire or a pauper; wanted or despised; a victor or a captive.

Your words can be filled with faith that will stir heaven and make men want you.

Remember that you can fill your words with love so they will melt the coldest heart, and warm and heal the broken and discouraged.

In other words, your words can become what you wish them to be.

You can make them rhyme. You can fill them with rhythm.

You can fill them with hatred, with poison; or you can make them breathe the very fragrance of heaven.

Now you can see vividly what your confession can mean to your own heart.

Your faith will never register above the words of your lips.

It isn't so bad to think a thing as it is to say it.

Thoughts may come and persist in staying, but you refuse to put them into words and they die unborn.

Cultivate the habit of thinking big things, and then learn to use words that will react upon your own spirit and make you a conqueror.

Jesus' confessions proved to be realities.

Faith's confessions create realities.

Jesus confessed that He was the Light of the World. He was it. The rejection of Him has plunged the world into a new darkness.

He said He was the bread from heaven, and it is true. The people who have fed upon His words have never suffered want.

His words build faith as we act on them, let them live in us.

His words were filled with Himself; as we act on them, they fill us with Christ.

His words feed faith and cause it to grow in power in us.

The believer's words should be born of love and filled with love.

Our lips are taking the place of His.

Our words should never bruise or hurt, but should bless and heal.

Jesus was the Way, the Reality, and the Life.

We are taking His place, showing the Way, confessing the Reality, enjoying the Life.

You will never enjoy what you are in Christ until His love rules your lips.

Until we know our legal rights in the Family of God, we will never become outstanding in our faith life.

We should know that the Bible is made up of two legal documents: the Abrahamic Covenant and the New Covenant; and that Jesus' death was a legal death to meet humanity's legal needs; and that His sacrifice, His substitutionary work was accepted by the supreme court of the universe; and that man has a legal right to take Jesus Christ as his Saviour and confess Him as his Lord which gives him a legal right to Eternal Life, the nature of God.

This makes him a son, and as a son he has a legal right to his Father's protection and care.

He has a legal right to all that Jesus purchased for him in His redemptive work.

He has a legal right to the use of the Name of Jesus in prayer and when dealing with demoniacal forces.

He has a legal right to the Holy Spirit's indwelling.

All promises and statements of fact in the Word are his.

He has a legal right to a perfect Redemption from Satan's dominion, from sickness and disease, from poverty and want.

He has a legal right to stand in the Father's presence because Jesus has become his legal Righteousness, and he has legally become the Righteousness of God in Christ.

He has a legal right to heaven as his home.

This takes prayer out of the realm of doubt and puts it into the realm of absolute certainty.

Chapter The Fifth

FAITH IN YOUR OWN RIGHTS

THE New Creation is based upon legal grounds. You have come into the Father's family because you responded to His call.

You could never have gotten in there by your own efforts.

You had to be born of the Holy Spirit. You had to be re-created through the agency of the Word; for He says, "Of His own will have we been begotten through the Word." (James 1:18 and 1 Pet. 1:23).

It is the Father's will.

It is through the Father's Word.

It is by the energy of the Holy Spirit that Eternal Life has been given to us, and we have become New Creations.

Of His own will He brought us forth.

It is not of man. It is not of the will of the flesh; it is of the will of our own Father. (John 1:13).

Rom. 3:21-26 gives us the legal background of our Redemption. "But now apart from the law a righteousness of God hath been manifested, being witnessed by the law and the prophets; even the righteousness of God through faith in Jesus Christ unto all them that believe; for there is no distinction; for all have sinned, and fall short of the glory of God; being justified freely by his grace through the redemption that is in Christ Jesus: whom God set forth to be a propitiation, through faith, in his blood, to show his righteousness because of the passing over of the sins done aforetime, in the forbearance of God; for the showing, I say, of his righteousness at this present season: that he might himself be righteous, and the righteousness of him that hath faith in Jesus." (Marg.)

It is a Redemption that gives us the Righteousness of God on the ground of faith in Jesus Christ.

It is a Redemption that gives us perfect Justification freely by His Grace, through the Redemption that is in Christ Jesus.

Grace is the Love of God in action, in manifestation.

It is Love doing things for us. It was Love that caused the Incarnation. Love caused this Incarnate One we call Jesus, to go

on the cross and become Sin with our sin; become absolutely
Identified with us, not only as a man (which He did in the Incarnation and in His earth walk, but He became Identified with our
sin nature on the Cross.

God laid upon Him our iniquity.

"Him who knew no sin, God made to become sin." That is
a serious thing. The heart can hardly take it in. We were sinners,
but He was made Sin.

He was so identified with the devil that God said He was Sin.

He actually went the limit for man. Being sin He was judged
as Sin. He was condemned as Sin. He was sent to the place of
suffering where Sin should go.

There He suffered until the claims of Justice against us were
fully met. Then he was "Justified in spirit." "He was made alive
in spirit." He was actually made as Righteous as He was before
He was made Sin. (1 Tim. 3:16; 1 Pet. 3:18).

He was made so Righteous that He who had cried, "My God,
my God why hast thou forsaken me?" after His Resurrection
entered into the presence of the Father with His own blood and
sealed our Redemption.

"Nor yet through the blood of goats and calves, but with his
own blood, entered in once and for all into the holy place, having
obtained eternal redemption." (Heb. 9:12).

He was so Righteous that He could sit down in the Father's
presence as though He had never been Sin. On the ground of His
finished work, when you accept it, you are made a New Creation.

You become the Righteousness of God in Him.

You stand in the Father's presence as though sin had never
been. We have never been able to accept this even mentally, but
it is coming slowly to the consciousness of the Church as they
listen to the Word.

Rom. 3:26: "For the showing, I say, of his righteousness, at
this present season: that he (God) might be righteous, and the
righteousness of him that hath faith in Jesus."

God actually becomes our Righteousness the moment that we
accept Christ as Saviour and confess Him as our Lord.

Men don't appreciate this, but the moment that a man becomes
a New Creation, he can stand in the presence of the Father as
Jesus did in His earth walk.

He is only a babe, but he has a perfect Righteousness and a
perfect Redemption. That Redemption is God-wrought. That Righteousness is God Himself.

God paid man's penalty on legal grounds and met the demands
of Justice absolutely.

It is not a problem of pity. It is not a problem of a mother's love that overlooks a son's disobedience and rebellion, but it is the Supreme Court of the Universe dealing with our rebellion and our sin, dealing with it so effectually that it can never become an issue again.

Another great fact: The New Creation is based upon absolutely legal grounds.

In the first three verses of Eph. 2 He has shown the condition of natural man. "And you did he make alive, when ye were dead through your trespasses and sins, wherein ye once walked according to the course of this world, according to the prince of the powers of the air, of the spirit that now worketh in the sons of disobedience; among whom we also all once lived in the lusts of our flesh, doing the desires of the flesh and of the mind, and were by nature children of wrath, even as the rest."

Natural man is spiritually dead. He is subject to the prince of the powers of the air. He is a child of disobedience. He is by nature a child of wrath.

Eph. 2:12: "He is without God and without hope in the world." He had no covenant claims on God. He was a stranger to the covenant of promise. He was hopeless, Godless, spiritually dead, a child of the devil. That is the condition of lost man.

I know they do not like to have that told to them, but if they are not told, then they will never see the need of Eternal Life.

Eph. 2:4-5: "But God, being rich in mercy, for his great love wherewith He loved us, even when we were dead through our trespasses, made us live together with Christ (by grace have ye been saved)."

In the plan of Redemption, God recreated us by faith.

Tenth verse: "For we are his workmanship, created in Christ Jesus for good works, which God afore prepared that we should walk in them."

By faith God recreated us in the Recreation of Christ when Jesus was made Alive after He had been made Sin; in that Recreation was our Recreation.

All we have to do is accept it. The moment we accept it, it becomes a reality to us in the mind of the Father.

Now you can understand what it means when He says that, "He raised us up with Him." (Eph. 2:6).

When He was raised from the dead by God's faith, we were raised together with Him.

"And made us to sit with Him in the heavenlies in Christ Jesus."

We are seated now by God's faith at the right hand of the Majesty on High. Do you see what mighty faith the Father had?

He believed that humanity would respond to the tug of His grace. Thank God, we have done it!

In this He shows "the riches of His kindness toward us in Christ Jesus: by grace have ye been saved through faith; and that not of yourselves, it is the gift of God; not of works, that no man should glory. For we are his workmanship, created in Christ Jesus for good works." (Eph. 2:5-10).,

By faith He did all the work that is necessary for the Re-creation of the whole body of Christ.

By the Father's faith we were New Creations in the Resurrection of Jesus.

When He said that He made us to sit down with Him at the right hand of the Majesty on High, do you realize what that meant? That back yonder the Father's faith saw us perfect conquerors, perfect victors, enthroned by the side of His own Son at His own right hand.

I tell you, that was faith!

I have faith in my Father's faith, that this is made good in me. Now you can understand 2 Cor. 5:17-21.

"Wherefore if any man is in Christ, there is a new creation." The moment you accept Christ, you are in the New Creation. "The old things are passed away." This is the experimental part of it. "Behold, they are become new. But all things are of God, who reconciled us to himself through Christ, and gave unto us the ministry of reconciliation." This is the ministry of reconciliation for this world, that was redeemed from the hand of the enemy, but does not know it.

The Redemption is of no value to them as long as they are ignorant of it.

They cannot enter into those riches until we tell them.

Today God is not reckoning unto the world their trespasses. He has committed unto us the Word that is to reconcile them to the fact that they have been recreated in Christ Jesus in His substitutionary work.

All they have to do is accept Him as their Saviour and confess Him as their Lord, and they enter into this new thing called the New Creation.

We are ambassadors with this new marvelous message of Grace.

We are saying to men, "Be ye reconciled to God—all you need to do is come to Him. He is waiting for you."

Eternal Life is yours. Fellowship with Him and relationship

all awaits you. Hear what He says to climax it.

"Him who knew no sin, God made to become sin." Doesn't that break your heart? Doesn't that cause your heart to respond to a love like that? He was made sin to the end that you might become the Righteousness of God in Him.

This is masterful. You are led out of failure and weakness and sin, and Satanic relationship, into the New Creation where you have become partakers of the divine nature, actual sons of God.

God has made you Righteous so you can can stand in His presence just as though you had never been a sinner, just as though sin has never soiled you.

You stand there complete in Christ.

This belongs to you. This is your legal right, and you can receive it yourself. If you believe in the finished work of Christ in you, and you believe in all God has done for you, it is yours; but it is not yours experimentally until you accept Him as your Saviour and confess Him as your Lord.

You believe in your own rights in Christ. Then you are a conqueror.

Rom. 8:14-17 gives us an insight into sonship rights and privileges. "For as many as are led by the spirit of God, these are the sons of God."

You have become a son. You have received not the spirit of bondage again unto fear. You have been delivered out of that. You have received the spirit of adoption. You are crying now, "Father, my dear Father."

The Holy Spirit Himself is bearing witness with your spirit through the Word that you are a child of God.

If you are a child, then you are an heir of God, and a joint-heir with Jesus Christ.

You see, you are taking your place now. You are responding to His challenge.

Rom. 8:31-39 is the climax of this mighty truth. "What then shall we say to these things, (that I have given to you?)"

"If God is for us, who is against us?" God is for us. He is our Father now. "He that spared not his own Son, but delivered him up for us all, how shall he not also with him freely give us all things?"

How shall He not give to us as a Father, all that belongs to us as a son's inheritance, a son's rights in Christ?

Who shall lay anything to our charge now? We are God's elect. It is God who has declared us Righteous.

It is God who has made us Righteous. It is God who declared

He is our Righteousness in Christ.

Now to climax it, Jesus is seated at the Father's right hand as our great Intercessor, Advocate, and Lord in the highest seat of the universe, the head of the body, the New Creation.

The New Creation is seated there with Him. No one can bring a charge against us. No one can conquer us.

Then He gives us a category of all the things that Satan can do against a man. Rom. 8:31-37: "What then shall we say to these things? If God is for us, who is against us? He that spared not his own Son, but delivered him up for us all, how shall he not also with him freely give us all things? Who shall lay anything to the charge of God's elect? It is God that justifieth; who is he that condemneth? It is Christ Jesus that died, yea rather, that was raised from the dead, who is at the right hand of God, who also maketh intercession for us. Who shall separate us from the love of Christ? Shall tribulation, or anguish, or persecution, or famine, or nakedness, or peril, or sword? Even as it is written, For thy sake we are killed all the day long; We were accounted as sheep for the slaughter."

Then he shouts this: "Nay, in all these things we are more than conquerors through him that loved us."

We stand complete in His completeness. We are victors in His own victory.

Not What We Should Be—
But What We Are Now In Christ!

The modern Christian does not object to my telling what they need, or my telling what they should do or be, but they can't understand me when I tell them what they are in Christ. They think I am bringing a new philosophy, a beautiful error, that will lead them astray.

I remember when I first saw this, I said, "If this were only true;" and then I said, "If I knew how to make it mine."

I didn't know that it was mine.

I didn't know that "He had blessed me with every spiritual blessing in Christ," and when I read it, it didn't register.

I remember 1 Cor. 3:21 where He declares that all things are mine, whether the revelation was given to Paul, or Cephas, or Apollos, it was mine.

That everything that the Father wrought in Christ in His great Substitution belongs to the individual believer.

It makes no difference whether the believer is educated or uneducated; whether he is rich or poor, the boundless grace unveiled in Christ, belongs to everyone of us.

Phil. 4:13 is absolutely ours: "I can do all things in him who strengtheneth me."

That is mine.

I can do anything that is necessary to be done because of His ability that has been imparted to me.

Psalms 27:1: "Jehovah is my light and my salvation; Whom shall I fear? Jehovah is the strength of my life; Of whom shall I be afraid?"

Note that carefully: "Jehovah is my light." That is wisdom. That is ability.

He is my ability to use the knowledge of what belongs to me.

Now I am able to take advantage of what the Epistles tell me belongs to me.

He is not only my ability, but my salvation, my deliverance, my redemption.

I am as free from Satan's dominion in the mind of the Father as Jesus was when He arose from the dead, because His Resurrection has freed me.

I have become a partaker of His Resurrection the moment I become a New Creation. Col. 3:1: "If then you were partakers of Christ's Resurrection." (Conybeare)

The ability of God that was exercised in the resurrection of Jesus belongs to the believer today.

Notice Eph. 1:19-20. Let me give you a somewhat free translation: "I want to show you what the exceeding greatness of the ability of God on our behalf who believe. It is according to the working of the strength of his might which he wrought in the Christ when he raised him from the dead and made him sit at his right hand."

We have never grasped the significance of this.

The Father has given to us the ability that He exercised in the resurrection of Jesus.

Then we who have received Eternal Life, have in our possession today the resurrection power or ability of God.

I am convinced that before the Master returns, there will be groups of men and women who will recognize this and take their place and begin to show to the world a type of supernatural ability that will startle a sense-knowledge ruled world.

It is no idle thing to have God in you.

One day it seemed as though He were questioning me. He said, "Have I been so diminished, have I become so small and so weak and ineffectual that you can ignore Me?

He said, "The God who raised Jesus from the dead is dwelling in you and He has lost none of His ability or power."

When He enters your life to dwell there, He doesn't lay aside His glory and Majesty and might.

When God's Son took upon Him the garment of flesh, He laid aside some of His glory.

But when the Holy Spirit comes into you, He comes full-fledged. He is the same mighty Holy Spirit that raised Jesus from the dead.

Rom. 8:11: "And if the Spirit of him that raised up Jesus from the dead dwelleth in you, he that raised up Christ Jesus from the dead shall give life to your death-doomed bodies."

I like that translation. It is vivid. It is true.

Then I want you to begin to reckon on Him. I want you to say in the morning, "That mighty One is in me. He can put me over today. I can face any emergency. I can do all things in Him because He is my strength."

I can hear Him whisper, Isaiah 41:10: "Fear thou not for I am with thee. ("I am in thee.") Be not dismayed for I am thy (Father) God. I will strengthen thee; yea, I will uphold thee; yea, I am today all that you need: your helper, your wisdom, your strength, your ability."

You see, it is not what I should be. It is not what I can be.

It is what I am in Christ.

We are not trying to be righteous; we are.

We are not trying to be strong, for God is the strength of our life.

We are not trying to be wise ,because Jesus has been made wisdom unto us.

We are what He says we are, so we can do what He says we can do.

God's Superman

Jesus uttered some prophetic facts about believers.

Matt. 19:26: "But nothing shall be impossible unto God."

Jesus is uttering a fact, and here is its compliment: Matt. 17:21: "And nothing shall be impossible unto you."

Take this with Mark 11:24: "Therefore, I say unto you, All things whatsoever ye pray and ask for, believe that ye have received them, and ye shall have them."

Or take Mark 9:23: "All things are possible to him that believeth."

The word "believeth" means "a believing one."

There were no "believing ones" in the time while Christ was preaching. They were Jews under law.

The "believing ones" came into being at Pentecost.

It meant a believer, a New Creation Man.

The new creation man is a partaker of God's nature.

He is really an Incarnation. He has received the nature and life of God.

Then he invites the Spirit who raised Jesus from the dead, who came on the day of Pentecost, to make His home in his body.

This man not only has God's nature, but has God actually living in him.

If this doesn't constitute a superman, then I don't know what a superman is.

But I am going to carry you one step farther.

This man with God's nature, and God dwelling in him, is given a legal right to the use of the Name of Jesus with the power of attorney.

The question is: What is that Name worth? What authority is there back of it?

Matt. 28:18-20 Jesus said: "All authority hath been given me in heaven and on earth. Go ye therefore, (with this authority) and make disciples, (or students), of all the nations; teaching them to observe all things whatsoever I have commanded you: and lo, I am with you always, even unto the end of the age."

You see what we have now?

We have the power of attorney to use the Name of Jesus; and all authority in heaven and on earth is invested in that Name.

Go over it just once more.

The believer is a new creation. The old things of weakness and failure have passed away and behold the old man has become a new man and all these things are of God. (2 Cor. 5:17.)

This man is a partaker of the divine nature, Eternal Life.

"He that hath the Son hath the life."

He has the Son—he has the life.

Now he has the Holy Spirit indwelling him. "Greater is he that is in me than he that is in the world."

This believer, this new creation, is a child of Deity.

He stands before the world as a very branch of the vine.

He is taking Jesus' place in the world.

And if this isn't a superman, then I don't know the meaning of the term.

The Church has kept this "Samson" imprisoned by false teachings and by creeds and doctrines. They have not only held him a prisoner to their philosophies and dogmas, but they have actually put out his eyes.

But the Father is going to restore sight to him and break the bonds that hold him.

The bonds of false teaching are going to be broken, and this child of God, this superman, is going to come into his own.

He has two formidable enemies. The worst one is Sense Knowledge. (Read, "Two Kinds of Knowledge.")

Entrenched in all our universities, colleges and technical schools, backed up by the press and religious periodicals, the great mass of the ministry are the devotees of the achievements of the Senses in the realm called Science.

And this superman in Christ has been held in bondage by them. They are the jailers.

The Father is calling for His sons and daughters to come out of the foxholes of fear and doubt, and meet their enemies in open combat.

Satan can no more conquer this body of Christ when it knows its rights, than he could conquer Jesus on the day of the Resurrection.

We are partakers, sharers in His Resurrection.

Hear Way, Col. 3:1: "If then ye have shared in Messiah's resurrection."

You see, we were raised together with Him in the mind of Justice.

We possess resurrection ability.

You doubt it? Read Acts 1:8: "But ye shall receive power when the Holy Spirit comes upon you."

The word "power" comes from the word "dunamis."

Young translates it "ability." "Ye shall receive ability when the Holy Spirit has recreated you."

Eph. 3:20: I have given you this Scripture several times in this book: "Now unto him that is able to do exceeding abundantly above all that you ask or think, according to the power (or ability) that abideth in you."

If that doesn't make supermen out of common men, then the English language cannot convey God's thought.

The problem is this: How long are we going to be held in bondage by Sense Knowledge?

How long are we going to refuse to take our place as the sons of God?

How long are we going to be intimidated by the fears and doctrines of men, while the Word of God is ignored?

To them, it is a root out of dry ground. To most of the people it has been a useless vine, something they could hang their doctrines and creeds upon.

It is coming to be to us what it really is in the mind of the Father.

Here is the Spirit's challenge: that you who read this, take your rights in prayer!

Begin to act like sons of God.

You have all heaven back of you.

You have the very angelic forces to do your bidding.

God is your strength and ability.

All things are possible to you because you are daring to act on the Word of God.

You are daring to live as Jesus dared to live in His earth walk.

You are the righteousness of God—that makes you a master of Satan; that gives you access to the throne; that permits you to take your place as a victor, as a spirit-warrior, as a conqueror.

You can have the consciousness that you are taking Jesus' place.

2 Cor. 2:1 is becoming a reality in your own life: "Thank God it is he who everywhere leads me in Messiah's triumph procession. By me he wafts abroad through me in every land the knowledge of Jesus. The incense is of his triumphal march." (Way's Trans.) And you can shout, Yes, I am Messiah's incense upwafted to God in the sight of all.

I am a master in His Name, with His ability.

I can do what He planned the Church should do, for I am what He says I am.

God's Real Man

Spiritual things are as real as material things.

Spiritual forces are stronger than mental.

Spiritual forces govern disease.

Spiritual forces govern natural laws.

Satan caused the wind on the Sea of Galilee. Jesus caused it to be still.

The believer in his contact with material, spiritual and mental forces, is as Jesus was in His earth walk—He is a Master.

The believer is a new creation, created by God Himself.

He has God's nature, Eternal Life.

Jesus is made unto him wisdom.

God is his strength.

The Holy Spirit is his ability.

He has the love nature of God so that he does not and cannot act like common men.

Love makes him like Jesus.

He has the mind of Christ and the ability that Christ had in His earth walk.

This makes him a superman.

God gave to him a legal right to the use of Jesus' Name which has all authortiy in heaven and on earth; which has authority over all the laws of nature, over every demon and his work, over all spiritual forces as well as material.

That authority and that ability belongs to the believer.

The recreated man is supernatural.

He is a superman.

Then why live in the senses, seeing, hearing, feeling, tasting and smelling!

All the knowledge natural man has, came through these channels to his brain.

We have Revelation knowledge.

What men of faith this truth will make!

What men of prayer will arise and take their place in Christ!

Here is the foundation on which to build a Prayer Life.

Many times our theologians have been our enemies.

They have made a philosophy of the truth; turned the Word into dogma and creed when it should have been as though the Master were here speaking to us.

The Word should speak to us as He would.

It takes His place.

It has the same authority as He would have if He were here.

When we pick up the Bible it would be good to remember that it is the book with God in it; Life in it; a God-indwelt book.

The spoken word in Paul's lips at Ephesus stirred the whole city. Acts 19:20: "So mightily grew the word of the Lord and prevailed."

It was not the written word, because up to that time the four Gospels had not been written. What epistles Paul had written were not in circulation.

It was the spoken word; yet it prevailed over that heathen city.

The written word today does not prevail in the church.

We read it, expound it, and the people go away and forget it.

In Acts 12:24, "The word of God grew and multiplied."

It was the spoken word in that city.

We should meditate in this Living Word until it becomes a reality, until it will be as though the Master stood in the room and spoke to us.

When Jesus met the disciples on the way to Emmaus, their testimony was, "Was not our heart burning within us, while he spake to us by the way, while He opened to us the scriptures?"

His word should have the same effect today upon our hearts.

The hush that they felt then should be upon our spirits now.

This can only come by meditation.

We sit in the presence of the tremendous realities of His combat against the hosts of darkness during His Substitution, of His mighty victory over the hosts of darkness, of His breaking the bonds of Death conquering the enemy that has ruled humanity ever since the fall, and that is credited to us.

It is as though we did it.

Satan knows he is defeated.

All heaven knows he is defeated.

And yet the church looks upon him as a Master.

Chapter The Sixth

THE INTEGRITY OF THE WORD

HE integrity of the Word is the basis of faith.

The reason for unbelief and a faltering faith is a lack of assurance of the integrity of the promises in the Word. In Rom. 10:8 it is called "the Word of faith."

God's Word gives birth to Faith: it is God's faith expressed.

Heb. 11:3: "By faith we understand that the worlds have been framed by the word of God, so that what is seen hath not been made out of things which appear."

In other words, this universe of ours came into being fresh from the womb of our Creator.

All God did to create was to say, "Let there be" and there leaped into being the things that are!

You see, God and His Word are one.

He named Jesus "the Word." "In the beginning was the Word, and the Word was with God, and the Word was God. The same was in the beginning with God. All things were made through him; and without him was not anything made that hath been made." (Jn. 1:1-3)

God linked Himself with His Word.

He made Himself a part of It.

He is not only in His Word, but He is back of His Word.

You cannot separate Him from His Word.

Gen. 22:16-17: "By myself have I sworn that in blessing I will bless thee, and multiplying I will multiply thy seed as the stars of the heavens and the sands upon the sea shore."

This was God's promise that backed the Abrahamic Covenant.

No wonder that man had confidence, and that we have this description in Rom. 4:17: "A father of many nations have I made thee, before him whom he believed, even God, who giveth life to the dead, and calleth the things that are not, as though they were."

He not only called the things that are not, and they leaped into being, but He watches over His Word to see that not one word fails.

In Rom. 4:18 speaking of Abraham He says, "Who in hope believed against hope, to the end that he might become a father of many nations, according to that which had been spoken. So shall thy seed be."

Now notice the next verse: "And without being weakened in faith he considered his own body now as good as dead, (he being about 100 years old), and the deadness of Sarah's womb; yet looking unto the promise of God (the spoken word), he wavered not through unbelief, but waxed strong through faith, giving glory to God, and being fully persuaded that what he had promised, he was able also to perform."

You can understand that when that angel spoke to Abraham it solved the problem.

Abraham never tried to believe; he simply acted on the word of that heavenly visitor.

Heb. 7:22 is one of the unknown scriptures that every believer should understand. "By so much also hath Jesus become the surety of a better covenant."

God, who was the surety of the old covenant said, "by myself have I sworn;" and He tells us in Heb. 6:17-18: "That he interposed with an oath; that by two immutable things, in which it is impossible for God to lie, we may have strong encouragement, who have fled for refuge to lay hold of the hope set before us."

Abraham rested on the angel's word.

Now we rest on this Living Word given to the Apostle Paul through the Holy Spirit.

Jesus is the guarantor for every word from Matthew 1:1 to Revelation 22:21.

All heaven is back of the Word; the very throne of God is back of the Word; and Jesus and the Father are back of the throne. They are all a part of this Word.

Jn. 1:14: "And the Word was made flesh, and dwelt among us."

This was the eternal "logos," the very Son of God.

Jesus said in Jn. 16:28: "I came out from the Father, and am come into the world: again, I leave the world, and go unto my Father." That was the Word who was made flesh.

Then in the New Covenant, the Four Gospels, and the Epistles God puts Himself into man's words.

Man had learned to communicate. Evidently God had given him his language. Now God is putting Himself into this word.

And if you remember I Thes. 2:13, all of the modern translators give us, "And for this cause we also thank God without ceasing, that, when ye received from us the 'spoken word,' the message, even the Word of God, ye accepted it not as the word oɪ men, but, as it is in reality, the Word of God, which also worketh in you that believe."

You understand that 1 Thessalonians was the first book written in what we call the New Testament. All they had had up to that time was "the spoken word." When Paul preached, his message was as authoritative as when he wrote; so he says, "you accepted this Word that I preached, not as though it were the word of a man, but as it really was, the very Word of God, and that Word that I preached to you worked in you; (the Spirit built it into your life so that it became a part of you)."

Here are some facts about the Word.

The Word is always Now.

It has been, it is, and it will be, the voice of God.

It is never old. It is always fresh and new.

To the heart that is in fellowship with the Father, the Word is a present-tense, living voice from heaven.

The Word is like its author: Eternal, Unchanging, Living.

Jesus was a root out of dry ground to His enemies. His revelation is a root out of dry ground to the skeptics of this day.

But it is a revelation of Love to His friends and to those who love Him.

Heb. 4:12, Moffatt's translation, "The logos of God is a living thing, active, more cutting than any sword with a double edge, penetrating to the very division of soul and spirit, joints and marrow, scrutinizing the very thoughts and conceptions of the heart."

And now notice this next sentence, "And no created thing is hidden from Him. All things lie open and exposed before the eyes of Him with whom we have to reckon."

Of what is He speaking? Of the Living "logos" that I hold in my hand; and He says that there is no creative thing hidden from the eyes of this Living Word, but all things lie open before Him.

This is a staggering thing to see that this Word is taking Jesus' place. It has all the elements in it that were in Jesus.

Reason will take the Word's place if we allow it to. Acting upon the Word doesn't appeal to the senses. The senses call acting on the Word "fanaticism."

The senses war against the Recreated Spirit holding it in bondage, refusing to act on the Word; and until the mind is renewed, the Word will never have its place in the believer's life.

Reason must give place to the Word.

The reason often robs the Word of its authority.

When I know that His Word is as authoritative today as it was when it fell from His lips, then it will be a living thing in my lips.

The Father's Word in Jesus' lips accomplished things. It hushed the sea. It quieted the wind. It raised the dead. It fed the multitudes.

His Living Word in lips of faith will do the same today.

When you know that the Word is God speaking, you will speak the Word with authority.

You remember that Faith in God is faith in His Word.

You want to build your Faith? Feed on the Word; act upon it.

You remember Matt. 4:4: "Man shall not live by bread alone, but by every word that proceedeth out of the mouth of God." You can't build faith and feed on any other kind of food.

Unbelief in the Word is unbelief in Him, the Author of it.

Our attitude toward the Word settles everything. You remember that man's word gives faith in man. God's Word when unveiled gives faith in God.

The word of a man is what man is. The Word of God is what He is.

Luke 1:37: "No word from God shall be void of power." That is what the angel said to Mary about the birth of Jesus, and Mary answered back, "Be it unto me according to thy Word."

If I could help believers to say that to the Master today, "Be it unto me according to thy Word," they would shake this modern age to its foundations.

Another translation that I like better, "Nothing is impossible to the Word of God." The Word in your lips can be as mighty as the Word in the Master's lips.

You remember that Jesus said again and again, "The words that I speak are not my words." John 12:49: "For I speak not from myself; but the Father that sent me, he hath given me a commandment what I should say, and what I should speak."

You have in this New Testament the Words of the Father.

You understand that the Four Gospels give a picture of what Jesus thought of His Father.

Jesus is introducing the Father.

He is trying to make the God of the Jews, the God of Abraham, and of Isaac and Jacob, known to the Jewish heart as a Father-God.

John 19:7 shows us that Jesus was crucified because He called God His Father. They had stoned Him for it. They had persecuted Him for it. Now they kill Him for it.

The Pauline Revelation is the Father introducing Jesus in reality.

He is introducing to us His substitutionary sacrifice that He wrought in His Son.

Not only that, but He is introducing the New Creation. It is a revelation of His sons and daughters here in a crooked and perverse world.

The Word in Jesus' lips was a living fact. What Jesus said was, is, and ever will be.

When we come to know that the Word was Jesus, the Word is Jesus speaking, then we will dare to speak it with confidence.

Then, He had just died and risen from the dead, but it is as fresh today as it was then. Jesus is of the "Now" as though He died last month and Pentecost was last week.

He is all this, Now. His Word is this living message to us, Now.

What He said was a part of Himself. The reality of it is throbbing in us, flows through us; our lives are governed by it. The Word was real; the Word is real. This is the foundation for Faith, and Faith gives substance to prayer and makes prayer a living reality.

Now soak in the Word. Let the Word work in you. John 15:7: "If ye abide in me, and my words are living in you, ask whatsoever ye will, and it will leap into being, it will become a fact." (Lit. Tr.)

The Living Word in our lips will be like the Spoken Word in Paul's lips.

The Father's Word in lips ruled by Faith, will be like His Word in Jesus' lips.

It is His Word that does things!

His creative ability is in His Word today.

His Word awaits the lips of faith.

This will make a prayer life like Paul's; it will give boldness to enter the Holy Place.

Is He Speaking To Me?

A miner lay dying in his shack in the hills of California. A Christian woman read to him John 3:16. He opened his eyes and looked at her. "Is that in the Bible?"

And she said, "Yes."

"Does it mean me?" He lay quiet a bit and then said, "Has He said anything else?"

And she read John 1:12: "And to as many as received him, to them gave he the right to become the children of God."

Then she answered softly, "Yes, He is speaking to you."

And the man opened his eyes and whispered again, "I accept him. I am satisfied." Then he passed on.

A Christian said, "I wish I knew whether He meant me when He gave us Isaiah 41:10: 'Fear thou not for I am with thee. Be not dismayed for I am thy God. I will strengthen thee; yea, I will help thee; yea, I will uphold thee with the right hand of my righteousness.' Did He mean me?"

Jer. 33:3: "Call unto me and I will answer thee and show thee great and fortified things which thou knowest not."

Is He speaking to me? Is He asking me to call unto Him?

Isaiah 45:11: "Ask me of the things that are to come concerning my sons, and concerning the work of my hands command ye me."

Is He speaking to me? Can I claim that as mine?

John 15:5: "I am the vine and ye are the branches." And the seventh verse: "If ye abide in me and my words abide in you, ye shall ask whatsoever ye will, and it shall be done unto you, (or another trans., it shall come into being)." Was that written for me? Does it mean that I can call unto Him anytime, anywhere, and He will hear me?

Does 1 John 5:14-15 mean me today? "And this is the boldness which we have toward him, that if we ask anything according to his will he heareth us; and if he heareth us, we know we have the petition that we have asked of him."

Yes, these are all yours.

It is as though you were the only person in the world and He was writing it for your special benefit.

"Hitherto ye have asked nothing in my name! Ask, and ye shall receive that your joy may be made full."

That is yours. There is no question about its belonging to you. It is as much yours as that check that was made out to you and signed by that business man. That is your check. You can get it cashed down at the store.

But that check is no more yours, than are these promises in this wonderful Book.

So take your place. Begin a real prayer life; you can do it; He is your helper.

Rom. 8:26: "The Spirit also helpeth our infirmity for we know not how to pray as we ought; but the Spirit Himself maketh intercession for us with groanings that cannot be uttered."

Let Him lead you into this prayer life.

He is always there to teach you.

He can open the Word and reveal your rights in Christ.

So act today!

The Word is the Father speaking to you.

It is not an old book that has a record of His message to men of ancient times; but the Bible, like its Author, is always Now.

And looking down through the ages He saw you, and this is written for your special benefit.

When He said, "I watch over my word to perform it," He was talking to you so that you would never question His Book again.

When He said, "If ye abide in me and my words abide in you, ye shall ask what ye will and it shall be done unto you," that is His present-tense message to your heart.

You can take it as though you heard it over your radio, fresh from His lips, as though He were speaking through a "mike" up yonder at the right hand of the Father, and that message came into your room and your name was called.

You knew it was for you.

Well, it would be no more yours than this scripture I have just given you.

When He said, "Whatsoever ye ask of the Father in my name, he will give it you," He meant it for you in your daily walk, in your prayer life.

While you are reading this now, it is the Father speaking to you.

It is as though He stood in the room and said: "Whatsoever ye ask in my Son's name, I will give it you."

Or if He said: "In my Son's name you may cast the demon out of that person, or you can lay hands on that person and they will be healed."

That Name is yours to be used any time, any place.

Remember this is not a religion; this is your personal contact with the Father. Your ability to pray and get results can't be questioned.

It is as real as though you were the only person for whom Christ died.

And when He says, "Him who knew no sin, he made to become sin, that we might become the righteousness of God in him," that means you.

When you accepted Him and received Eternal Life you received His righteousness, and you became that very moment a New Creation.

You became at the same time, the righteousness of God in Him.

He doesn't have to do anything else—it is all done.

The work is finished.

The New Creation is a fact.

All you need to do now is to act as though you knew it to be true, just as you act on any other fact of life.

We will assume that you are working in a factory and you are notified by the management that your pay has been raised. You at once plan what you will do with that new income.

As you sit here reading this, you remember that the Great. Mighty Holy Spirit who raised Jesus from the dead is in your body.

He is there to cooperate with you.

You are to cooperate with Him.

That Greater One is in you with His resurrection power and ability.

You act on it.

You don't try to have faith. Faith is unnecessary now because He is in you, and this all belongs to you.

You have to have faith for things that do not belong to you.

The thing that is yours, is yours, so Now you will act on the Word without fear or questioning!

The Father's Word In Your Lips

"For I spake not from myself; but the Father that sent me, he hath given me a commandment, what I should say, and what I should speak." (John 12:49)

This is a marvelous statement from the lips of the Master.

50th verse: "The things therefore, which I speak, even as the Father hath said unto me, so I speak."

Jesus declared that He came down out of heaven not to do His own will but the will of Him that sent Him.

The works that Jesus did, He declared were His Father's works.

He said, "For what I see the Father doing, that do I also, in like manner."

The miracles that Jesus performed were the Father's miracles.

The marvelous words that He spoke were the Father's words.

Now you can see the power of the Father's words in Jesus' lips. Jesus knew who He was. He knew He was the Son of God. He knew God was His own Father. He knew that He came out from the Father. He knew He was going back to the Father. He knew His place and His work.

He was never vaccilating in His actions or in His speech. There was a positive element in His messages that thrilled the heart.

There was a quiet assurance in every step. He took His place and acted the part of a Son.

He continually confessed His Sonship and His mission in the world.

As I face this fact, I ask myself this question: "Can we have the same assurance today, the same positiveness that Jesus had?"

Yes, a thousand times, yes!

We are Redeemed from the hand of the enemy.

Col. 1:13-14: "Who delivered us out of the authority of darkness, and translated us into the kingdom of the Son of his love; in whom we have our redemption, the remission of our sins."

That is a declarative statement in regard to our place, our standing and liberty in Christ.

We have been delivered out of darkness. We have been translated into the kingdom of the Son of His love.

We are Redeemed; our sins have been wiped out. Then we haven't anything to do with bondage nor with our past life, for when we were recreated it tells us in 2 Cor. 5:17-18: "Wherefore if any man is in Christ, he is a new creation: the old things are passed away; behold, they are become new. But all these things are of God, who reconciled us to himself through Christ, and gave unto us the ministry of reconciliation."

We know that we are recreated and that Satan has no dominion over the New Creation.

We know that we are reconciled to the Father. That means a perfect fellowship.

We know that if we are reconciled we can come into His presence without condemnation.

We know that with that reconciliation has come Righteousness, the ability to stand in the Father's presence without condemnation or inferiority.

Jesus had no more than that.

Jesus had no sin-consciousness. We have no sense of sin.

Jesus had no sense of unrighteousness. We have no sense of unrighteousness, because we have been declared Righteous with His own Righteousness by the very living Word of God.

Jesus had no better Righteousness than we have, because God is our Righteousness.

Jesus had no better fellowship than we have, because our fellowship has been wrought by God, Himself.

Jesus had no better right in prayer or any more power in dealing with demons than we have.

All authority was given to Jesus, and He gave us a legal right to the use of His Name.

If the Word means what it says, we have a standing with the Father, we have rights and privileges which we have never taken advantage of.

There is no sense of reality, no sense of God in the modern church.

John 7:29: "I know Him; because I am from Him and He sent me."

John 8:54-55 is Jesus' positive confession about His relationship with the Father.

"It is my father that glorifieth me; of whom ye say, that He is your God; and ye have not known Him: but I know Him; and if I should say, I know Him not, I should be like unto you, a liar: but I know Him, and keep His word."

We can know the Father. We can know our sonship rights.

He is my Father; I am His child; I am in His family.

Jesus said He came down here to do the Father's will. When we confess the Lordship of Jesus, we confess our purpose—to do the Father's will.

He said, "Be not ignorant but understand what the will of the Father is." (Eph. 5:17)

Let us form the habit of thinking that His will for us has more joy in it than anything which is contrary to His will.

Let us educate ourselves in the consciousness that His will is best; that His will has permanent joy and gladness in it; His will has success in it.

Outside of His will is confusion, unhappiness and misery.

Jesus walked in love.

"Greater is he that is in you that he that is in the world." The One who is in you is Love.

God is Love.

"For it is God who is at work within you." You have Love in you. You have God's nature in you. You have God, Himself, in you.

We are dealing with realities. Most of our preaching is theory, speculation, telling us what we ought to do and be.

The only difficulty is that we have never confessed what we are in Him!

Jesus continually confessed what He was. Modern teaching has made it almost a crime to acknowledge what we are in Christ.

All that Jesus was to His Father in His earth walk, we may be to the Father in our earth walk.

We have the same Holy Spirit that Jesus had. We have the same words that Jesus uttered which were the Father's words.

In our lips today, we can have the very message that Jesus had.

The Pauline Revelation is the Word of the Father. We can fill our mouth with this Revelation of Paul's. We will be speaking the Father's words.

We will be taking Jesus' place in the earth, saying the Father's words just as Jesus did when He walked the earth.

What a prayer life awaits us!

Jesus knew Who He was. He knew why He came.

We may know who we are in Christ. We are New Creations created in Christ Jesus. We have His Nature.

There need not be anything mysterious about our walk. We may know exactly who we are. We may know why we are as Jesus did.

Jesus knew His Father. He said, "I came out from the Father; I came into the world. Again I leave the world and go unto my Father."

We may know our Father. We are born of God, and God is our Father.

We may know Him as really the Master knew Him.

If you start the day with Him, you will fellowship with Him. When you awaken in the morning you whisper softly, "Good morning, Father. Here is another day to live and walk with Thee."

Whatever problem confronts you, you consult Him in your heart.

If it is wisdom that you need, you thank Him for it. If it is love to meet a disagreeable situation, He is there in you to take you over and live His own Life through you.

He can make your words just like Jesus' words, full of love, full of sympathy, full of courage.

It would be good for you once in a while to stop and say to your Father, "Thank you for ability, for giving me wisdom to meet this problem."

Jesus in you is Authority over demoniacal forces and over the laws of nature.

We may know our ability. We may know that we have authority over all the demoniacal forces.

"In my name ye shall cast out demons."

"Greater is He that is in you than he that is in the world."

These are facts. We know them. We are not afraid to face life with the consciousness of victors.

In the morning you take stock. You say, "He and I are going together. I have access to His ability, His wisdom, His love, His grace, His strength to meet every issue that confronts me. I shall have physical strength for every need today. I shall have wisdom to meet every issue. I shall have love no matter what the provocation may be."

You see, when you walk like this, your prayer life becomes a realistic thing.

Jesus had no sense of need. There was always a sureness in all He did.

Well, if He is in me and for me, and I have His Word, there should be a sureness about my walk. I should not walk as a blind man, feeling my way along. I should walk erect. I should keep pace with the momentum of life around me. There should be an absolute certainty about my decisions.

When I remember that He is my sufficiency, it makes no difference what the problem may be; He is there. I have his guidance. I am assured of his presence, and He will not let me fail.

He was never discouraged, and He whispers to me: "Fear thou not for I am with thee; be not dismayed, for I am thy God. I will strengthen thee; I will uphold thee with the right hand of my righteousness."

That is mine. I fearlessly take up the task before me. Unconsciously I am living in His presence. I am walking in His presence. His eye of love is upon me all the time. He and I are carrying out His will.

Why, prayer just becomes a means of communication between He and I. It is not a slavish duty. It is not a difficult task. It is not hard work.

He and I are working together.

We have found that sonship without fellowship would neither satisfy the heart of the Father nor the heart of His Child.

Fellowship must be based upon absolutely sure grounds so the child may know that he can go into the Father's presence with the same freedom that your child enters your presence.

It must not be based upon grounds of pity or sufferance, but on the ground of love's own relationship.

The old idea of prayer doesn't fit into this new unveiling of love's ground work in redemption.

The Father is love, and He has given us His love nature, so fellowship is as natural as breathing.

The Word teaches us how to maintain our fellowship and how to regain it if we should lose it.

Fellowship with the Father is the very heart of a prayer life.

There can be no vigorous faith exercised without a rich fellowship existing between the two.

We may know that we are His children. We may know our legal rights, but if our fellowship has been broken it shatters our faith, and fills us with fear and dread.

Then maintaining our fellowship is one of the most important facts of this spiritual life

Chapter The Seventh

RELATIONSHIP AND FELLOWSHIP

HERE are two great objectives in Redemption. The first is relationship. God is working to the end that man may legally become His child, a partaker of His very nature, so that he will be a genuine heir and joint-heir with Jesus.

The second objective is to restore to man his lost Fellowship.

This can only come as Righteousness is restored to him. Job 33:26: "He restoreth unto man his righteousness."

There can be no fellowship unless man can stand in the presence of God the Father without the consciousness of guilt, of sin, or of inferiority.

There can be no fellowship of the type that the Father craves unless man is utterly free from sin consciousness and free from the fear of Satan's dominion.

So the whole Redemptive processes have been to the end that He might have children, and that these children should live in the closest fellowship of love and freedom with Himself.

Sonship, then, must be based upon legal grounds. There must be no question as to man's legal standing in the family of God.

The sin problem must be settled on legal grounds so that God will have a perfect right to impart to man His own nature, thereby making this man an absolute New Creation.

The sin in his nature must be driven out by the nature of God coming in.

His spirit must be in perfect harmony with the Father. Man is a spirit. The part of man that had to be recreated was the spirit of man.

His mind is renewed and his body brought into subjection to the Word.

That constitutes the first phase of a perfect Redemption.

Man must become an actual child of God, as truly as was Jesus in His earth walk.

This can only come by a re-birth of his spirit, a real New Creation of which Jesus speaks in Jn. 3:3-8.

"Verily, verily, I say unto thee, except one be born anew, he cannot see the kingdom of God .... Except one be born of water and the Spirit, he cannot enter into the kingdom of God. That which is born of the flesh is flesh; and that which is born of the Spirit is spirit. Marvel not that I said unto thee, Ye must be born from above."

Jas. 1:18 tells us that we are begotten of the will of the Father. "Of his own will he brought us forth by the word of truth, that we should be a kind of firstfruits of his creatures."

Two facts are shown here: We are born of His will. We are born of His Word. It is all of God.

Eph. 2:10: "For we are His workmanship, created in Christ Jesus for good works, which God afore prepared that we should walk in them."

That New Creation is all of God, wrought through the Word and of the Holy Spirit.

It is a God-planned and a God-executed relationship.

That New Creation is all of God. Man is actually a child of God, as that boy is a child of that man and woman.

As soon as he is Recreated, the Father begins the beautiful process of Renewing his mind.

Rom. 12:2: "And be not fashioned according to this age: but be ye transformed by the renewing of your mind, that ye may prove what is the good and acceptable and perfect will of God."

That word "transformed" comes from the same Greek word from which the word "transfigured" comes in speaking of Jesus' transfiguration on the Mount.

The renewing of the mind will be a transfiguration of our minds.

No one can overestimate this wonderful fact.

These minds of ours have been dominated by the Senses, so that all the knowledge that we have has been Sense Knowledge.

This mind is going to be renewed by the Spirit, and by our meditation in the Word and practicing of the Word, until our mind is in perfect fellowship with our recreated spirit and with the Word.

Few believers have a renewed mind.

Consequently, only a few of them ever get into the deep things of God, and their prayer life seldom becomes a reality.

Only a few of them know the riches of His grace.

1 Cor. 2:10-13 tells how the Spirit searches all things, even the deep things of God, so that we may know the things that were freely given to us of God. Which things also we speak, not in words which man's wisdom teacheth, but which the Spirit alone can give.

The renewed mind, coming into this deep, rich fellowship with the Father through the Word, is able to appreciate and understand the wealth of the Redemptive work that was wrought in Christ.

Eph. 1:3: "Blessed be the God and Father of our Lord Jesus Christ, who hath blessed us with every spiritual blessing in the heavenlies in Christ."

That falls dead upon the ears of the average believer; and yet, that average believer is a possessor of all the things that Christ wrought in his Redemption.

He has been blessed with every spiritual blessing in Christ.

Christianity is the Life of God imparted to a man, plus the wealth of the riches of God's nature which is imparted to us, and the Spirit's unveiling of the wealth of God that was revealed in Christ in His Redemptive work.

It was a faith-provoking thing, a love-stimulating thing.

It revolutionizes the intellect; it thrills the spirit.

It lifts a man out of the natural into the supernatural.

When his mind is renewed on the basis of his sonship rights, he can take his place as a son.

He can enjoy a son's rights and privileges. He can assume a son's responsibility and step into all the riches of the grace of God.

This comes when man loses his sin consciousness, his sense of inferiority.

He never does this until he knows about Righteousness.

The church is so woefully ignorant of Righteousness today. She thinks Righteousness only means doing right deeds.

But in the Revelation He gave to Paul, Righteousness means the ability to stand in the Father's presence without a sense of guilt, inferiority, or sin, just as free in the Father's presence as was Jesus.

She thinks we will have to wait until we die before this is possible.

It is ours now, in this present, evil world.

Right here now we may have as sweet fellowship and communion with the Father as Jesus had in His earth walk.

Heb. 9:9, speaking of the gifts and sacrifices under the First Covenant says, "That cannot as touching the conscience, make the worshipper perfect."

The blood of bulls and goats could only cover sin, and the scape goat could only bear sins away typically.

But when the fulness of time came, and Jesus put sin away by the sacrifice of Himself, then Heb. 9:14 became a reality: "How much more shall the blood of Christ, who through the eternal Spirit offered himself without blemish unto God, cleanse your conscience from dead works to serve the living God?"

Heb. 10:1-3, speaking of the First Covenant, says: "The law having a shadow of the good things to come, not the very image of the things, can never with the same sacrifices year by year, which they offer continually, make perfect them that draw nigh. Else would they not have ceased to be offered? Because the worshippers, having been once cleansed, would have had no more consciousness of sins. But in those sacrifices there is a remembrance made of sins year by year."

There was nothing perfect about the Old Covenant.

When He came, He made one sacrifice for sins forever. (Heb. 9:26) Then He sat down on the right hand of the Majesty on high.

He had put away sin by the sacrifice of Himself. He had made the New Creation possible.

He made Remission of Sins possible. All the sins we committed were remitted, wiped out as though they never were.

That New Creation is to be free from sin consciousness so that the believer is no longer held in bondage to Satan's condemnation.

Rom. 8:1 becomes a reality: "There is therefore now no condemnation to them that are in Christ Jesus."

Rom. 8:33: "Who shall lay anything to the charge of God's elect?" It is God who has declared them Righteous.

God Himself has done it.

2 Cor. 5:21: "Him who knew no sin, he made to be sin on our behalf; that we might become the righteousness of God in Him."

We not only have Righteousness reckoned to us, and Righteousness imputed to us, but we have had Righteousness imparted to us in the New Creation.

Eph. 4:24: "And put on the new man, that after God hath been created in righteousness and holiness of truth." We have been created out of Righteousness and holiness of truth.

That thrills the heart.

The very fact of a New Creation and of sonship demands a perfect Righteousness.

Could you think of a son who could not stand in his Father's presence? Sonship would have no meaning, no significance whatever.

We have now a perfect relationship. God is our very Father; we are His very sons and daughters.

Our relationship cannot be challenged because it is based upon the finished work of Christ.

God has wrought it Himself.

When we accepted Christ as our Savior and confessed Him as our Lord, then God Himself, through the Word, by the Holy

Spirit's energy Recreated us, imparting to us His own nature, Eternal Life.

Jn. 6:47: "He that believeth hath eternal life."

1 Jn. 5:13: "These things have I written unto you, that ye may know that ye have eternal life, even unto you that believe on the name of the Son of God."

Jn. 5:24: "He that heareth my word, and believeth him that sent me, hath eternal life, and cometh not into judgment, but hath passed out of death into life."

The death out of which he has passed is spiritual death, union with Satan.

He has passed out of that, by being born out of it.

Now he is in the realm of supernatural Life.

Rom. 5:17, (Weymouth's trans.): "For if, through the transgression of the one individual, Death made use of the one individual to seize the sovereignty, all the more shall those who receive God's overflowing grace and gift of righteousness reign as kings in Life through the one individual, Jesus Christ."

Here we get the whole picture: Through the abundance of grace and the gift of Righteousness we reign as Kings in the realm of Life—as conquerors, as overcomers.

That is a triumphant strain right from the heart of the Father, not to become a fact only in Heaven, but right here and now.

Fellowship

Fellowship is based upon Righteousness. Fellowship means "sharing together."

Marriage is a good illustration. It is partnership. It is getting under the burden as one.

It is an equal exchange, both giving of their best. Another word that it suggests is "communion."

That means "The two are pouring into the same cup," and they become perfectly one in the blending just as God says, "The two shall become one flesh."

That is fellowship. Jesus said, "I am the vine; ye are the branches."

Our fellowship with the Father is based upon relationship.

Fellowship between husband and wife is based upon relationship.

Fellowship is the one thing that makes married life beautiful.

The law that binds the man or woman together does not make fellowship.

It is not the fact that the woman is a good cook and housekeeper, or that the man is a splendid provider and a gentleman at all times.

It is when that man and woman are blended together into one, spiritually, physically, and mentally.

That is communion. That is real fellowship.

We often have in our home life a limited fellowship. In the church we have a limited fellowship with the brethren; that means we also have limited fellowship with the Father.

It is unlimited fellowship that brings happiness into the home. It is unlimited fellowship with the Father and with one another that brings the richest, deepest joy into the believer's life.

1 Cor. 1:9: "God is faithful, through whom ye were called into the fellowship of his Son Jesus Christ our Lord."

We were called into fellowship with His son.

This is a heavenly calling.

We are to bear the burdens of Jesus, in bringing a lost world to the knowledge of the truth.

We are fellowshipping Jesus when we go to Africa, or India, or China as a missionary.

We are fellowshipping Jesus when we fellowship the missionary who goes with our money and prayers.

Fellowshipping means giving.

I fellowship the missionary by sending him my offerings.

I have been called into this fellowship of Jesus, and now I am fellowshipping the Master and carrying out His will in the world.

The New Birth and Righteousness are to one end: That we may enjoy the sweetest fellowship with the Father and with the Son.

Fellowship is the parent of Real Faith. If you find someone whose Faith is weak, you may know that his fellowship has been broken, or it is of a low type.

Fellowship between a husband and wife can be easily broken. The marriage is not broken. It takes the court that married them to do that.

This broken fellowship does not break your relationship, but it mars it and robs that relationship of its richest blessings and benefits.

All low grade faith comes from a low grade of fellowship.

Most Christians have lost their fellowship and are putting duty in the place of it.

They are like a husband and wife whose fellowship has been broken.

The husband brings home presents that only bring tears to the eyes of his wife.

She does not want the presents. She wants fellowship restored.

Broken fellowship is one of the saddest facts of human experience.

Here is a couple who have lived in absolute heaven. Then an unkind word or a thoughtless act has marred their lives.

They are both too proud to acknowledge the fault, and the gulf between them becomes almost impassable because they are unwilling to ask each other's forgiveness.

The Holy Spirit has given us the way to restore broken fellowship in the epistle of John.

This short epistle was written to tell us how to maintain our fellowship and how to restore it when it is broken.

1 Jn. 1:3-4: "That which we have seen and heard declare we unto you also, that ye also may have fellowship with us: yea, and our fellowship is with the Father, and with his Son Jesus Christ: and these things we write, that your joy may be made full."

Joy cannot be made full without full fellowship.

"And this is the message which we have heard from Him and announce unto you, that God is light, and in him is no darkness at all. If we say that we have fellowship with him and walk in the darkness, we lie, and do not the truth." 1 Jn. 1:5-6.

God is light, and as long as you are in fellowship with Him, you are in the light.

But the instant your fellowship is broken, you go into the dark.

Hatred is darkness. That hatred has blinded our eyes. I Jn. 2:11: "But he that hateth his brother is in the darkness, and walketh in the darkness, and knoweth not whither he goeth, because the darkness hath blinded his eyes."

This man is out of fellowship. He is walking in darkness. He does not know where he is going.

How many Christians are like that! They refuse to walk in the light of the Word.

That means walking in love. Every step out of love is a step into the dark.

"If we walk in the light, as he is in the light, we have fellowship one with another, and the blood of Jesus his Son cleanseth us from all sin." 1 Jn. 1:7.

As long as we walk in the light, the blood of Jesus Christ cleanses all the blunders and mistakes that we make.

"But if we say we have no sin—" when we have broken fellowship, and are walking in the darkness, "we deceive ourselves, and the truth is not in us. If we confess our sins, he is faithful and righteous to forgive us our sins, and to cleanse us from all unrighteousness." 1 Jn. 1:8-9.

This scripture is not written to the world. It is written to the church, the family of God.

It has to do with broken fellowship.

The instant that you confess your sins, that instant He is faithful and Righteous to forgive you.

Now you are to forgive yourself and forget your sins and go on in love with Him.

For you to continually remind yourself of your past errors and sins is to deny the efficacy of His forgiveness and the value of His Word.

1 John 2:1: "My little children, these things write I unto you that ye may not sin. And if any man sin, we have an Advocate with the Father, Jesus Christ the righteous."

Jesus is the Righteous Advocate. He can go into the Father's presence when we are under condemnation and shrink from meeting Him.

He is always Righteous. He can always plead our case.

The instant we ask the Father's forgiveness, Jesus takes up our case before the Father and our fellowship is restored.

There is no need of walking in broken fellowship a minute after you have committed sin.

The Devil is the author of that sin.

Then to walk on in broken fellowship, grieving over your blunder, is only adding joy and glory to the Devil.

The instant you have done wrong and your fellowship is impaired, ask the Father's forgiveness and go on in fellowship with Him. 1 Jno. 1:9, 2:1-2.

Restoring fellowship is restoring joy, restoring power with God.

The richer the fellowship, the deeper one gets into the Word.

Deep, rich fellowship means that we go far below the surface in this mine of wealth.

You cannot walk in love without fellowship.

To walk in love is to walk in fellowship.

To live the love life is to live the fellowship life.

It is bringing joy to the heart of the Father.

It is the sweetest, biggest, richest thing the world ever knew, this fellowship life with Him.

The church knows very little about it. Almost no one ever preaches about it, yet it is the heart of the whole thing.

There can be no growth in faith, or growth in grace, or growth in knowledge, or growth in joy, with broken fellowship.

Every person that has lost power with God has lost it through loss of fellowship.

If their faith has been impaired so their prayer life is but a form, it is because fellowship has been broken.

If their joy has all seeped out, it is because the vessel that held it has been cracked; their usefulness and testimony has lost its grip and power, it is mere empty words; it is because fellowship has been broken.

If you want your testimony rich and full, then you must have fellowship that is rich and full.

There are three things that characterize fellowship. You are taking advantage of your Righteousness.

You are bearing the fruits of Righteousness.

What are those fruits? You are now able to pray with the sick, cast out demons, open the scriptures, lead lost men to Christ with unspeakable freedom.

There is joy in this life in Christ.

When you are walking in Righteousness, you are walking as Jesus walked when He was on earth.

There is fulness of joy. It is the joy of Christianity that makes Christianity the most attractive thing in the world.

When joy goes, the Word loses its power, its freshness and richness.

It is only when fellowship is at flood tide, and we are walking in the fulness of Righteousness, that God is honored and souls are saved.

A third thing, there will be no development of faith. There is the Word: it is just as rich and full today as it ever was, but somehow or other the lips seem paralyzed.

There is no longer light on the Word. The sick cry for help, but find no release because fellowship is broken and faith is slowly ebbing away.

Fellowship in its fulness is the joy life with the throttle wide open on a down grade.

Fellowship in its fulness is the soil out of which living faith grows to fruition.

Faith dies on a low type of fellowship.

It shrivels up.

It is like a desert plant.

By taking your place in Righteousness, you will find joy in the Word, freedom to use the Name of Jesus, and conquering faith will master every circumstance that confronts you.

Then the maintaining of a rich, full fellowship is vastly important.

Col. 3:16: "Let the Word of Christ dwell in you richly."

That is the key. It is the Word dwelling in us in all its fulness, its variety, its beauty, its graciousness that produces a rich type of fellowship.

It will give place to love. It will produce all the fruits of Righteousness. Faith cannot grow rich on any other soil.

A rich prayer life depends on your Fellowship.

You must be in Fellowship or you can't enjoy the throne of grace.

If your Fellowship is broken, you know what to do to have it restored.

You can't afford to stay in the dark; too many issues are at stake.

To know that Satan is defeated by our Substitute, and that his defeat is eternal, makes our Redemption a blessed reality.

To know that that defeat was administered to him by our Substitute, and set to our credit, so that in the records of the supreme court of the universe we are the masters of Satan, and that Satan recognizes that in the Name of Jesus we are his rulers—when the heart knows this as the body knows heat and cold, then faith is unnecessary.

It is simply a fact that we have come to know; and we act upon that knowledge as we act upon the fact of the ground being able to sustain our weight.

We know that God Himself put Satan and all his ability beneath our feet, and that we are looked upon by the Father, and by Satan, as a master of the dominion of darkness.

We are taking Jesus' place.

We carry out in our daily walk the things Jesus would have done could He have been in our place.

He came to destroy the works of the Adversary.

We are completing the work that He began.

Then arise and take your place; act the part of a son; assume your responsibilities.

Dare the impossible: His Name can't fail you!

You are a victor; He made you one; get used to it, so you can play the part.

Make your confession harmonize with the facts.

You are what He says you are in Christ.

Remember His Word is truth (or reality).

Launch out boldly on the Word!

Chapter The Eighth

HE PUT ALL THINGS IN SUBJECTION
UNDER HIS FEET

IN the first three chapters of the epistle to the Ephesians, we have the consummation of Christ's substitutionary work in regard to Satan and demons.

Paul prays that "our eyes may be opened or enlightened, that we may know what is the richness of the glory of his inheritance in the saints, and what the exceeding greatness of his ability on our behalf who believe." (Eph. 1 :18-23)

He fairly shouts that, "It is according to that working of the strength of his might which he wrought in the Christ, when he raised him from among the dead."

He declares the same ability that wrought in the dead body of Jesus when He was raised to immortality, is at work within us.

The heart can hardly take it in that the same Might, the same Resurrection Power that wrought in the dead body of Jesus is ours today.

"And if the Spirit of him who raised up Jesus from the dead dwelleth in you, he that raised up Christ Jesus from the dead shall also quicken (or heal or strengthen) your mortal bodies." Rom. 8 :11.

"And he made him to sit at his right hand in the heavenlies, far above all rule, and authority, and power, and dominion, and every name that is named, not only in this age, but also in that which is to come."

You must always keep in mind that we were raised together with Him, and He made us to sit with Him in the heavenlies; so representatively, we are seated on the throne with Christ.

He is the head of the body.

We are members of that body.

So if the head is exalted, the body is exalted with it.

If He has been given all authority, that authority belongs to the Church, His body. It is for the benefit of the Church.

If He conquered all the forces of darkness and left them paralyzed and broken before He arose from the dead, it is as though we had accomplished that mighty work.

It is all reckoned to us. set to our credit.

When will our hearts take it in, and our minds become fruitful with this mighty unveiling of what we are in Christ today!

Notice carefully the twenty-second and twenty-third verses: "And he put all things in subjection under his feet, and he gave him to be head over all things for the benefit of the Church."

We are His body—then all these malign and wicked influences are beneath our feet.

We are masters of them all.

He did not defeat them for Himself. He defeated them for us.

He did not fight that battle for His glory, but for our good.

Adam had sold us out in his sin of high treason.

Jesus redeemed us, defeated our enemy and put him beneath our feet.

When will the heart take it in?

That knowledge should become as common to us, and as usable as the multiplication table. Someone must pioneer it; begin to teach it.

Hear the next sentence: "He gave him to be head over all things for the benefit of the church, which is his body, the fulness of him that filleth all in all."

We are the fulness of Him.

John 1:16 says: "Of his fulness have we all received."

The same thing is brought out in Col. 2:9-10: "For in him dwelleth all the fulness of the Godhead bodily, and in him ye are made full, who is the head of all principality and power."

He is not only our fulness, but we are His fulness.

The word, "fulness" comes from a Greek word that is almost untranslatable: "pleroma." which means "completeness," "perfectness," or any other synonym that suggests fulness.

We have received of that fulness. That fulness has filled us.

Can't you see what masters we are of demoniacal forces?

They are beneath our feet.

"But thanks be unto God, who always leadeth us in triumph in Christ." (2 Cor. 2:14)

That is the hallelujah chorus of the New Creation, and it never becomes real until we begin to confess it, begin to tell to the world what we are in Christ.

Heb. 9:12 tells us that this is an Eternal Redemption. Not just a redemption for the hour in which it was done, but that Satan is as much defeated now as he was when Christ arose from the dead; that he is as much a subject to the Name of Jesus as he was when Jesus conquered him.

In writing to the Corinthian Church, 1 Cor. 2:6 (Moffatt's Trans.): "We speak wisdom, however, among them that are fullgrown; it is not a wisdom of this age, nor of the rulers of this age who are dethroned," in their master and head, Satan. This wisdom for the fullgrown is something that we need to know about.

The great body of the Church are in their infancy; they are mere babes in Christ.

Many of our leaders have never passed beyond that. They are still dominated by the senses. They are big men in the sense realm!

Sense knowledge has taken the Church captive, bound our leaders and holds them captive.

Very little is known of "spiritual wisdom and revelation in the knowledge of him."

Col. 1:9-12 is almost utterly unknown: "That we may be filled with the exact knowledge of his will in all spiritual wisdom and understanding."

Let's have that. That belongs to us.

There will never be a struggle after faith again.

Your prayer life will be like the Master's.

The sense of unworthiness that comes from sin-consciousness would be destroyed in that full knowledge, that "exact and perfect knowledge," of our redemption and righteousness in Christ.

He says we need this in order "to walk worthily of the Lord unto all pleasing, bearing fruit in every good work, and increasing in this exact knowledge of God, made powerful with his ability, according to the might of his glory, unto all steadfastness and longsuffering with joy."

What mighty men of God that would make!

Notice the twelfth verse: "We will be giving thanks unto the Father who has given us the ability to enjoy our share of the inheritance of the saints in light." (Lit.)

We have passed out of the babyhood state, out of the adolescent period, into full manhood and womanhood in Christ.

What prayer bands it would make, when we know the reality of the thirteenth and fourteenth verses: "Who delivereth us out of the authority of darkness, and translated us into the kingdom of the Son of his love; in whom we have our redemption, and the remission of our trespasses."

Notice what that means. If you are conscious of a perfect redemption from Satan's dominion, you will walk with a sureness that Jesus had in His earth walk.

That sureness comes from knowing that everything you had ever done, and all that you ever were, stopped being at the New Creation.

All of your past has stopped being. You start anew.

Then if you make mistakes, you have the intercession of Jesus.

All you have to do is acknowledge your mistake and it is wiped out instantly, and your fellowship is restored.

You have been delivered out of the authority of Satan. Satan has no authority or legal right to reign over you.

You are the absolute master of Satanic forces in the Name of Jesus.

You are now in the kingdom of the Son of the Father's love.

We are masters there.

We are conquerors.

I want you to see that you hold exactly the same position that Paul held, and you have a right to do as is recorded in Col. 1:28-29: "Admonishing every man and teaching every man in all wisdom, that we may present every man perfect in Christ." He is speaking here of the New Creation man.

Now notice the 29th verse: "Whereunto I labor also, striving according to his working, which worketh in me mightily."

"For it is God who is at work within you, willing and working his own good pleasure."

You see this combat is not ours. It is His combat. He did it for us.

He is doing a mighty work in us, and a mighty work through us in helping others.

In Eph. 1:3-7 is a picture of a God-planned, and a God-executed Redemption and New Creation. It is a God-sized work.

"Blessed be the God and Father of my Lord Jesus Christ, who hath blessed me with every spiritual blessing in the heavenlies in Christ."

Now notice: "He chose us in him way back before the foundation of the world, that we should be holy and without blemish in his presence; having in love foreordained us into the position of sons through Jesus Christ, unto Himself."

Go over that again.

Let it soak into your very being that way back yonder before the foundation of the world God planned to have us. We are the products of that plan.

And when the fulness of time came, He said to the great heathen world: "Whosoever will, may come and become a member of my foreplanned family."

It is "Whosoever will," and you have answered that call; you are a member of that holy body that can stand in His presence without the sense of guilt or condemnation.

You have been blessed with every spiritual blessing—that was purchased in the redemptive work of His Son.

It is all yours.

These riches require no faith to enjoy.

They belong to us as much as the money that was given to us by some loved one.

He tells us in the sixth verse that: "It was freely bestowed upon us in the Beloved."

Not grudgingly, not scantily, but it was according to the riches of His grace.

Notice the seventh verse: "In whom we have our redemption through his blood, the remission of our trespasses, and it according to the very riches of His love, the riches of His glory, the fulness of His grace."

How can you be a weakling?

How can you act like the ignorant and untaught?

Can't you see your place now?

You must glorify Him by taking your place in Christ.

Never think of faith again. This all belongs to you.

Never think of your worthiness, for He is your righteousness.

Don't think of your ability, because He is your ability.

Swing free then.

Come out into all the fulness of His marvelous grace.

Enjoy your rights and take your place and fill His heart with joy.

"And he raised us up with him, and made us to sit with him in the heavenlies, in Christ." (Eph. 2:6.)

Think of yourself as seated with Him.

We do as Paul did when he cast the demon out of the insane girl: "In the Name of Jesus, come out of her."

How we should praise Him for this ability!

We are masters.

We are overcomers.

We reign with Him.

Can't you see what a background this is for a prayer life that will shake the very throne of darkness?

Think of your enemies as beneath your feet, conquered, defeated.

Stop your trying.

This is grace. All is yours.

Take your place.

Circumstances drive us to God in prayer.

The Word gives us faith to come boldly to Him.

His Name assures us that He hears our prayer.

They are filled with malignity and hatred, and will seek to make it unpleasant for you, but you are master of them.

You don't have to fight them.

Your fight is a faith fight, described in Eph. 6:12: "Our combat is not against flesh and blood, but against principalities and powers, the world rulers of this darkness.

We are their masters, and we conquer them with words.

Jesus cast out demons with words.

He healed the sick with words.

He hushed the sea with words.

And He gave us the ability to use words, His words, His own Name that has all authority.

Thus we do as Peter did at the Beautiful Gate of the temple: we say, "In Jesus Name, rise and walk."

Forgetteth What Manner of Man He Is

"He goeth away, and straightway forgetteth what manner of man he is." (James 1:24)

The New Creation man, unless he has made a careful study of what he is in Christ, in the time of stress or a crisis will forget what "manner of man he is."

We have lived so long in the realm of the senses that it is difficult for us to realize what we are in Christ.

We unconsciously lapse into the old life, seeing ourselves as we were, and not as we are.

Eph. 1:7-9 is not a workable reality for many: "In whom we have our redemption through his blood, the remission of our trespasses, according to the riches of his grace, which he made to abound toward us in all wisdom and prudence, making known unto us the mystery of his will, according to his good pleasure which he purposed in him."

This Scripture is almost an unknown quantity.

Note the first sentence: "In whom (that is, in Christ) we have our redemption" from Satan's dominion, from Satan's authority, for "we have been translated into the kingdom of the son of his love;" and Jesus has become our new Lord, our love Master He is our caretaker, the guarantor of our ability to reign over the forces that once dominated us.

We have (a present-tense fact) our redemption from fear and the cause of fear, and we are now not only delivered, but we have become masters where once we were held in bondage.

There has been a remission of all our past trespasses, and that remission has been according to the riches of His grace.

That is an unfathomable expression of love.

Who knows what "the riches of His grace" means to us! And He made this abound toward us in all wisdom, for Christ has been made wisdom unto us.

That is a strange expression. We have the wisdom to face life's problems with prudence, and this wisdom and prudence and ability of God is His will toward us.

At first I couldn't take it in. Then I saw it.

I am His son. I must act the part of a son. I must take the place of a son. I must do the work of a son.

Then I'll need prudence. I'll need wisdom. I'll need His ability to face every contingency.

This is something I possess. I need no faith to obtain it. Prayer is not necessary, for it is mine.

How often since this possession came to me I have forgotten what manner of man I was.

For the moment I have acted like a "mere man" as Weymouth puts it; a very babe.

Sense knowledge throws her dark mantle over my spirit, and I forget Him and His ability.

I forget the Name and its authority.

I forget that "greater is He that is in me than he that is in the world."

And I question for a moment.

Then He brings back to me what I am in Christ, and I joyously take my place.

Oft-times we forget our righteousness. "He has made us to be his righteousness in Christ."

The Adversary would make us forget this, and sense knowledge would cause us to doubt our worthiness and our ability to stand in His presense.

It would make us say, "Oh, if I only had faith," when faith is not needed, for "He has blessed us with every spiritual blessing in Christ."

We are rich with His riches.

We are strong with His strength in the inward man.

We should make it a business to affirm constantly what we are in Christ. Every believer should make out a list on a little card or in a notebook of what he is in Christ. Then read it over and over.

Start with the fact that: In Him I have my redemption.

In Him I am a New Creation, and Satan has no dominion over me.

Jesus alone is my Lord.

I am the righteousness of God in Christ.

I have as much a right in Jesus' presence, or as much a right in the Father's presence as Jesus has in His presence.

And I have a standing invitation to the throne room to come boldly and take my place as a son. I need to remember this so that I will never disgrace Him by acting like a "mere man" or by forgetting what manner of man I am.

I should remind myself that I have fellowship with Him; that I am a sharer in the burdens He has, as He is a sharer in mine.

I should remind myself that I am a member of the fruit-bearing body of Christ.

I should never allow myself to forget what manner of man He made me.

I should remember that "It is God who is at work within me, willing and working His own good pleasure."

That takes me out of the old life. I may be in the old surroundings. There may be everything about me as it was before, but this inward man of the heart has been recreated.

The real man has been made in the image of my Father God; and I have the use of the Name of Jesus; and I have my Father's ability to meet life's problems as they are.

A prayer program should have a place in the Church as well as the Sunday School.

In fact no Sunday school can function properly that isn't backed by prayer.

A prayerless ministry is a powerless ministry.

Church history proves that the ministry of prayer makes the ministry of the Word a powerful thing.

We have thought that psychology could take the place of prayer, but it cannot; that education and culture could take the place of prayer, but our present church proves that we are wrong.

A prayerless church is a useless church.

It isn't functioning; it isn't meeting the needs of the congregation.

It is nothing better than a religious club.

Few people ever leave a deeply spiritual, prayer-ruled church to join in the philosophical religious cults of the day.

A prayerless church is a cold church, a sense-ruled church.

A prayerless pulpit where you hear nothing but empty words has no spiritual value, and does not minister to the needs of the spirit of man.

It should be prayer, and preaching, and teaching.

But we have changed it.

We have dropped prayer, and teaching of the Word, out of the program.

We have put preaching first, and we have classes in psychology and philosophy instead of teaching men how to pray.

There should be a department of prayer in every church. That should be the heating plant of the spiritual life, the very sinews of the church.

Chapter The Ninth

PRAYER AND THE CHURCH

EVERY church should have a Prayer Program.

There should be a prayer organization, as well as the young people's or the Sunday School organization.

The prayer life of the church should be so interwoven with every feature of it that God could be seen in every department.

The finances are called the sinews of the church, but this is not true.

Prayer forms the real sinews of the church.

You remember that the prayer life brings those who pray into vital contact with the Father, the Son, and the Holy Spirit, as well as continually in touch with the Word.

It isn't just saying prayers, but meeting Him for a while, getting His mind for the day, His strength, His quietness, and His love.

This vital contact has certain spiritual reactions that are of inestimable value to the life of the church.

We all know what it will mean when a great number of the people in the church enlist in a Prayer Program and come in vital contact with the Lord daily.

Every man and woman in connection with our church who is not spending time in prayer will be a neutralizing force in the church.

They may be in the choir; they may be in the Sunday School; they may have charge of the finances; they may act as deacons or elders; but whatever their place, they carry a certain coldness, they are an inert body.

They have a tendency to lower the spiritual temperature of everyone in close contact with them.

So it is vitally important that the largest possible number of the membership should be led into the Prayer Program of the church.

This isn't any place for theory.

This is the place for positive facts.

A church can't be built up spiritually without prayer.

Numbers can be drawn through personal work or by eloquence, but to build up a real spiritual body, is only possible through prayer.

This will need much wise teaching on the part of the Pastor, and the teachers of adult classes.

Give prayer a large place in your church program. Don't only teach about prayer, but practice it.

Have prayer services with a real program. Give subjects for definite intercession.

While one intercedes, train the rest to make that prayer theirs; not by shouting loud "amens," but silently making that intercession their very own.

The whole group will be crowding into the Throne Room, making that request as their own.

You can educate the people so that their prayers will prevail. Make them Prayer Masters, mighty in Intercession.

The Prayer Problem

The Prayer Problem is a problem of Faith; and Faith is a problem of the integrity of the Word, of the ability of God to stand back of His promises or the statements of fact in the Word.

There is another side of the problem: It is the ability of the believer to stand in the Father's presence without the sense of guilt, condemnation or inferiority.

The real question then, is after we know that the Word cannot be broken and that God keeps it to the very letter, "Have I a right to stand in the Father's presence and make my petitions known to Him without condemnation?"

Here are a few things that every believer should know.

First, that we are actually New Creations, created in Christ Jesus. 2 Cor. 5:17: "Wherefore, if any man is in Christ there is a new creation, the old things are passed away; behold, they are become new. But all these things are of God, who reconciled us to himself through Christ."

Notice these facts, that "if any man is in Christ." One is in Christ once for all. He doesn't enter Christ and then leave Him. If he leaves Him, it is final.

The second fact: He is a New Creation, a new species.

He has received into his spirit the life and nature of God.

The old things are passed away.

These old things are Spiritual Death, his union with Satan, and his old sins—the sins committed while he was spiritually in union with the Adversary. These are remitted.

A new self is given to him.

The old self, or the old man stops being; for the old self, or the old man as it is called, cannot live in Christ.

Notice again: "If any man is in Christ he is a new creature, a new creation, and the old things are passed away."

That New Creation is the product of God.

It is created in Christ Jesus.

It is born from above.

It is born of the Holy Spirit, through the Word.

And that new thing stands uncondemned and reconciled before the Father.

2 Cor. 5:21 states it clearly: "Him who knew no sin he (God) made to be sin on our behalf; that we might become the righteousness of God in him."

The moment that we become New Creations, we become the righteousness of God.

The righteousness of God means the ability to stand in the Father's presence without the sense of guilt, condemnation or inferiority.

We are that moment Sons and Daughters of God.

It would be an abnormal thing if He should recreate us, impart to us His own nature, and leave us under the blighting curse of condemnation, unable to stand in His presence without the sense of guilt and inferiority.

Then we know we have the ability to stand in God's presence free from all sense of unworthiness.

We know the second fact that we have a legal right in the Father's presence because we are legally born into His Family, and He has legally adopted us and accepted us as Sons. "The Holy Spirit Himself has born witness with our spirits that we are the children of God."

We know another fact, that we have a legal right to the use of Jesus' Name and whatsoever we ask of the Father in that name He'll grant us.

This has cleared up every issue in regard to our ability to stand before Him in the throne room without condemnation.

Sin has been preached to us so long and we have been told so often that we are unworthy and unfit, that it has kept us with a sense of inferiority which has been destructive to a faith life.

No man can walk with God as long as he is under condemnation.

You can see now that prayer is based on legal grounds; not based on promises only but on statements of fact.

It isn't a problem then of faith with the believer, for all things belong to him. Eph. 1:3: "Blessed be the God and Father of our Lord Jesus Christ who has blessed us with every spiritual blessing in the heavenlies in Christ."

You cannot grasp this too clearly that it is not a problem of faith with us as sons and daughters of God.

It is merely a problem of our taking our place, enjoying our rights.

"He has blessed us with every spiritual blessing."

Then everything that was wrought in the finished work of Christ belongs to us. It is our own property this moment.

All our struggling to get faith has been the result of ignorance of what belonged to us.

Now we must simply take our place, use our rights.

But someone says, "What about the struggle with the Adversary?"

Yes, we have war with a defeated enemy.

Satan was defeated before Jesus arose from the dead.

Read my book "Identification" and it will prove to you that we were crucified with Christ, died with Christ, buried with Christ, suffered with Christ, justified with Christ, made alive with Christ, conquered the Adversary with Christ, and then were raised together with Him, and now we are seated together with Him.

That shows us our utter oneness and union with Christ.

It shows what our combat with the Adversary was when we conquered Satan with Christ before He arose from the dead.

Everything that Jesus did is accredited to us.

The entire substitutionary work of Christ was for us.

He didn't conquer Satan for Himself.

He didn't put sin away for Himself.

He didn't suffer the judgment that would have fallen upon the sinner for Himself.

But He suffered it on our behalf, and we have entered into His victory; it is accredited to us. So Satan now is a defeated enemy.

We war not with flesh and blood, not with humans, but with demons who know that we are, in Jesus' Name, their Masters.

Every demon knows that you, the recreated one, are his master.

They rule us by subterfuge, by bluff, by deception.

They put diseases upon us and hold us in bondage through our ignorance of what we are in Christ and what belongs to us.

Have Your Own Faith

One should never trust the great issues of his life to another's faith. He should have faith of his own, faith that can meet any crisis that may come.

Your case is vital to you. It may not be vital to this other party to whose faith you look. He may have troubles that are unsolved, inward struggles that have never been settled. His faith may be at a low ebb when you appeal to him for aid.

It is vitally important to you that you have your own faith to fall back on in these hard places.

Everyone should build his own faith life.

I find that the majority of people float on carelessly until they come to a dangerous place. They are sick, or some loved one is sick, some financial or heart problem confronts them that may affect their entire future. Then they frantically hunt for someone who can cry and sob and quote scriptures in what they call their "prayer" and it is of no avail because there is no faith back of it.

If there was faith there, there would be no crying and no sobbing. There would be a rejoicing because they would know that whatever they ask of the Father in Jesus' Name, He will do it.

Here are some facts that will help you to begin to build your own faith life.

The Word is yours. It is as though there was no other person in the world but you, and this Revelation had been given especially to you; you can say, "It is mine. No one has a better right to it than I have. Every promise is mine. Every statement of fact is mine."

When He said, "Whatsoever ye shall ask of the Father in my name, he will give it to you," you can say, "He was talking to me.

"He is my Father; I am His child. This is His message to me, to help me in my earth walk. Jn. 15:7 was given by the Master from the Father to me for He said, 'The words that I speak are not mine, but the Father is speaking through me.'

"Consequently it is the Father who said, "If ye abide in Christ, and His words abide in you, ask whatsoever ye will, and it shall be done unto you. Herein am I glorified, that ye bear much fruit.' This is prayer fruit. It is going to be borne by one of the branches, and I am that branch."

When your heart can speak like this, then you know that when you approach the throne of Grace there is a willing ear, listening to you, and whatever you ask (because the Word is living in you) you will receive.

Do you understand what that means? A lover has written you a letter. It is not written to anyone else. It is too sacred for any other eyes to see. That is your letter. That is your lover writing to you.

God is love and He has written to you the book called the Bible. Jesus came to unveil love, and the revelation of love is given to us in the Word.

Jesus now has spoken a love message to you. He says, "If ye abide in me." If you are a New Creation, you certainly do abide in Him. His words abide in you just as that lover's words would abide in your heart.

You go over that lover's words again and again. He has asked you to become his companion for life. How sacred is that letter. It is love's own message to your heart. Love has spoken to you.

Love says, "If ye abide in me, and my words have found their place in you, you can ask what you will, and I will see that you get it."

The Holy Spirit Is Yours

The Holy Spirit belongs to you.

Luke 11:13: "How much more will your heavenly Father give the Holy Spirit to them that ask Him?" Only sons and daughters will ever ask Him.

You are His child. You have received His very nature. You are as really His child as was Jesus when He walked in Galilee.

Then you have a right to the Spirit. You can ask Him to come in and make His home in your body; as surely as you ask Him, so surely will He come in, because "No Word from God is void of an answer." The Word of God is very sacred to Him.

Jer. 1:12: "I watch over my Word to perform it."

This is His message to you. It is the lover again speaking to His beloved and saying, "Do you wish the Holy Spirit to make His home in your body? If you do, just invite Him in, for He is standing at the door awaiting your invitation. If you ask Him in, He will enter, then guide you into all the reality of the finished work wrought by Jesus."

More than that, you can confidently say, "His Righteousness is mine for He was made unto me Righteousness. I have become, through the New Birth, the very Righteousness of God in Christ.

My Righteousness is just as good as Jesus' Righteousness because it is Jesus' Righteousness. It is just as good as Paul, or Peter, or John had. No one has a better Righteousness than I." When I realize that, faith is no longer a problem.

The Word is mine. The Holy Spirit is mine. Jesus is mine. God is my own Father. Their Righteousness is my Righteousness. I stand complete in their completeness.

"I am a New Creation, created in Christ Jesus. All the rights and privileges of a child are mine. I did not have to ask for them. They were conferred upon me. When I became His child, these things were a part of the New Creation so I enter into my rights.

Satan's Defeat

"One of the greatest blessings, one of the most wonderful facts is that Satan was defeated for me.

"Jesus' victory over him is my victory.

"When I was Redeemed in Christ, that Redemption was out of the hand of the enemy.

"I have been translated out of the kingdom of Satan, into the kingdom of the Son of the Father's love; in whom I have my Redemption, complete and perfect.

"Then I do not have to war to conquer Satan, because Satan is already conquered.

"He was conquered for me. He knows that he was conquered for me, so I take my deliverance from him and my victory over him in Jesus' Name, with thankfulness.

"I know that Satan is the author of disease and confusion and heart suffering. I know that Jesus said, 'In my name ye shall cast out demons.' When Jesus said that, He was saying it to me. He was talking to me personally.

"He said, 'In my name you shall cast out demons. Do you understand what that means to you?'

"I said for Him to tell me. He said, 'It means that you, personally, rule Satan, and his works—that demons are subject to you. Just as demons are subject to me, and disease and physical needs, and financial needs are all subject to me, they are to you.

" 'Remember how I paid Peter's poll tax? Remember how I fed the multitudes? Do you remember how I walked upon the sea? Do you remember how I turned water into wine? Now I am turning over to you this authority over the adversary.

" 'Not only that, but I am turning over to you the ability to use this authority, for ability has been given unto me in heaven and on earth. Now I want you to use this ability. I am turning it over to you. That ability will teach you how to use this authority that has been delegated to you to use my name. In this ability is my wisdom, my ability.

" 'The Holy Spirit is to bring that ability into you through my Word. You go now and use this delegated authority with my own ability, for I am your sufficiency to meet every need and every crisis of your life.' "

It is just as though Jesus stood in the room and said this to you. Not only this (and it seems as though this were enough), but He has given you a legal right to the use of the Name of Jesus.

You can say, "I have the power of attorney to use the Name of Jesus. Jesus declared that all authority in heaven and on earth were His. That authority then is enwrapped in the Name. It is a part of the Name, and He has given me a legal right to use it— the power of attorney.

"Now I can destroy the works of the adversary. I can set men free. Now I can break the power and dominion of disease and demons over the bodies, hearts and minds of men.

"Now I can actually take Jesus' place and do His works. I can understand what He meant now when He said, 'Greater works than these shall ye do because I go unto the Father.' I have His own Word for it.

"I have the same Spirit who raised Jesus from the dead within me.

"I have the same Righteousness that Jesus had, because He is that Righteousness.

"I rejoice in the fact of Satan's defeat on my behalf.

"I have the Name of Jesus. God is my own Father. What more could I ask? But that is not all. I am His own child. I do not have to try to be His child. I am. I am born of His Spirit. I am a partaker of His nature, Eternal Life.

"His Word has given me absolute assurance of my relationship with Him; so fearlessly I make my confession to the world. I am a child of God. I am a New Creation. I am an heir of God, and a joint-heir with Jesus Christ.

"He loves me even as He loved Jesus. His home is my home. When I finish my work here, if Jesus tarries, I will go to my Father's home for it is my home.

"These great soul-thrilling facts have given birth to a real faith in my own heart.

"I have my own faith now. I have confidence in my faith. I know that whatever I ask of the Father in Jesus' Name He will give it to me. I know I have authority over all the authority of the enemy in Jesus' Name."

Our theological schools have never had a department on Faith, so every church should have a faith clinic, one class a week on the study and development of Faith.

Faith is not a product of sense knowledge.

It is not a product of intellectual faculties.

Faith is born of the human spirit.

Whether we want to face it or not, the fact is: there is no love in the natural human heart, and there is no faith in the natural human heart.

Faith and love spring from the recreated human spirit.

Until a man has received Eternal Life, the nature of God, he cannot be a faith man, and he cannot be a love man. He will only have a Sense Knowledge Faith.

God is a faith God.

Faith is His nature just as love is His nature.

I have sometimes thought that love was the mother of faith; that faith sprang out of the roots of love.

And love can only come from its source, the Father's heart.

So when we are Born Again, receive Eternal Life the nature of God, that nature begets in us faith, and we build our faith by feeding on God's Word.

His Word is the only source of strength for the recreated human spirit; the only source of building faith.

Faith cannot be built by abstract reasoning.

It is only built by my acting on the Word, letting the Word live in me as it did in Jesus.

By my doing the Word, I build faith in my spirit.
I become a doer of the Word, a practicer of the Word.

The Word becomes a part of my very being.

I absorb it in my daily life, and it builds into me the faith of God.

Chapter The Tenth

A STUDY IN FAITH

HE reason faith is so difficult is that Sense Knowledge has gained the ascendency in our educational and religious life. Sense knowledge has all come through our physical contact with the world.

We have learned to trust so utterly in our eyes, our ears, the sense of touch, of smell, and the sense of taste, that spiritual things are hard to understand.

It is easy to believe in things you see.

The crowd said about Jesus, "We see the miracles; now we believe in thee."

Thomas fell down at His feet when he saw the wounded side and the holes in His hands and feet. He said, "Lord, I believe." Jesus said, "Blessed are they who have not seen, yet believe." The Master touched the heart of things there.

Faith is independent of Sense Knowledge.

The antagonism of the scholastic world to the Revelation called the Bible is that the Bible demands faith in things the Senses cannot apprehend.

Heb. 11:3 tells us that the worlds have been framed by faith through the Word of God. "By faith we understand that the worlds have been framed by the word of God, so that what is seen hath not been made out of things which appear."

That explains the first verse, "Now faith is assurance of things hoped for, a conviction of things not seen," or "Faith is giving substance to things hoped for."

Hope is not faith.

Faith is always now.

Hope is always future.

God said, "Let there be," and the sun, moon, and stars came into being.

He said, "Let there be an earth," and the earth came into being.

He said, "Let there be light," and there was light. It was a warm light that encircled the whole earth and made it a subtropical garden, out of which have come our coal fields, oil, chemicals, and minerals.

Then He said, "Let the earth bring forth," and the earth brought forth.

"Let the animals come," and the animals came.

Faith is the mightiest force in the universe.

It is the creative ability of God.

It is the creative ability of man.

Animals act by instinct, not faith.

Man acts by faith.

Man was created in the image and likeness of the Faith of God.

He is created in the image of love. He is created in the image of faith.

Whether you recognize it or not, man's entire life, from the time he becomes conscious as a babe, until he steps off into the unknown, is a faith life; one has faith in his senses, the other in God.

When man loses faith, life has lost its objective.

Great financiers are faith men.

Woolworth had faith in five and ten cent pieces.

Ford had faith in an automobile.

Edison had faith in electricity.

Faith is the thing that brings success.

Doubt is the thing that brings failure.

The educational institution that teaches doubt becomes the unconscious enemy of civilization.

The modern trend of Sense Knowledge has been toward agnosticism.

The agnostic possesses the proud confession of "I do not know."

Atheism says that God does not exist.

The two of them are twin enemies of success and mental spiritual progress of the age.

The agnostic makes no contribution but confusion.

God is love. He works by faith. It is faith that works by love.

He is the faith God.

Man is the crowning work of faith.

Being created in the image of love, he must live by faith.

Man is a faith creation.

When reason usurps the seat of faith, man becomes a failure.

Let us now consider what faith in the spiritual realm can mean.

Some Realities

The bolder the faith, the greater is the success.

Faith wins.

When faith dies, success folds its wings.

We can take as the slogan of life Matt. 19-26: "But with God all things are possible."

Unite with Mk. 9:23: "All things are possible to him that believeth."

1 Jn. 4:4: "Greater is He that is in you, than he that is in the world."

Who is in you? It is God!

Then to the God who is within you, all things are possible.

If you give that God within you liberty, let Him loose in you, you become limitless in your realm.

"All things are possible to him that believeth." The Greek word there for "believe" means "a believing one."

That is a child of God, a believing one.

You and God are linked together. You become invincible.

You see a glimpse of this in Luther's ministry.

We saw it in John Alexander Dowie.

We have seen it in individuals here and there—God and man linked together, doing the impossible.

We know that every step out of love means sin.

We know that every step out of faith means weakness and failure.

The word, "believing," is a verb. The word, "faith," is a noun.

Believing is acting on the Word.

Faith is the result of this action.

Jesus acted on the Word of His Father. He said, "The words that I speak unto you are not mine but my Father's." Jn. 14:10.

All His works were a result of His words.

Matt. 8:5-13 gives us a record of the Centurion.

8th verse, "But only say the word, and my servant shall be healed."

Jesus spoke the Word.

The healing of the leper, the healing of the woman with the issue of blood, and the healing of the man mentioned in Mark 2:3-12 are miracles performed by His word.

Matt. 14:23-33 is the story of Peter's walking on the waves.

Peter said, "If it be thou, bid me come." Jesus simply said one word, "Come." When He did, the waters sustained the weight of Peter.

Again we see Jesus quieting the sea. It was words that quieted it. He simply said, "Peace be still." Mk. 4:35-39.

Jesus' faith was in His Word.

Acts 3:1-11 gives us a picture of Peter's faith in the Name of Jesus in his lips.

Sixth verse, "But Peter said, Silver and gold have I none; but what I have, that give I thee. In the name of Jesus Christ of Nazareth, walk." The life-long cripple became well and strong.

Acts 20:7-12 is the story of the young man falling out of the third-story window. He was taken up dead. "And Paul went down, and fell on him, and embracing him said, Make ye no ado; for his life is in him. And when he was gone up, and had broken the bread, and eaten, and had talked with them a long while, even till break of day, so he departed. And they brought the lad alive, and were not a little comforted."

It was the Name of Christ in the lips of Paul that raised the lad from the dead.

Faith, then, is acting and speaking the Word of God.

Sense Knowledge speaks the word of man, and faith speaks the Word of God.

Sense Knowledge man acts upon Sense Knowledge.

The faith man acts upon the Word of God.

Faith is giving substance to the thing that you had long hoped would become real.

Heb. 11:1, in one translation reads, "Now faith is the title deed to things hoped for."

Hope never gave a title deed, but faith is the title deed.

When you believe the Word, anxiety and fear leave you.

As long as you hope, you will be filled with anxiety and worry.

Mk. 11:22, "Jesus answering said unto them, Have faith in God," or "Have the faith of God."

It is Jesus' challenge for us to have the God kind of faith. He had it.

"Verily I say unto you, Whosoever shall say unto this mountain, Be thou taken up and cast into the sea; and shall not doubt in his heart, but shall believe that what he saith cometh to pass; he shall have it."

There are two things to notice: He believes in his heart, and he believes in his words.

You believe in your heart, and then you believe in the words on your lips.

That gives you power over demons and disease and circumstances.

Mk. 11:24: "All things whatsoever ye pray and ask for, believe that ye receive them, and ye shall have them."

They have not been in your possession, but it is just as real as though they were.

Faith counts the things that are not as though they were.

Rom. 4:17, Faith counted the things that were not as though they were and they became.

Abraham counted that Sarah was able to give birth to a child when she was ninety years of age, and she became the mother of Isaac.

Abraham believed that his body would be rejuvenated, and it was.

Rom. 4:19 is God's commentary on this.

"And without being weakened in faith he considered his own body now as good as dead (he being about a hundred years old), and the deadness of Sarah's womb; yet, looking unto the promise of God, he wavered not through unbelief, but waxed strong through faith, giving glory to God, and being fully assured that what He had promised, He was able also to perform."

You can see the resistlessness, the absolute ability of faith.

Faith in you will conquer as faith in Jesus conquered.

Faith in your own words will drive disease out of sick men's bodies .

When you say, "In the Name of Jesus, disease depart from this body," you have confidence in Jesus' words in your lips as Jesus had confidence in His Father's words in His lips, and the healing takes place.

Faith comes by daring to act upon the Word.

Your fear to act upon the Word is unbelief gaining the ascendency.

Matt. 18:18: "Verily I say unto you, What things soever ye shall bind on earth shall be bound in heaven; and what things soever ye shall loose on earth shall be loosed in heaven."

Here is God's challenge to united faith.

Everyone of you should hunt for a partner who can believe with you, who can unite his faith with yours.

You become a resistless power the moment you do.

You may be mighty in faith alone, but you can be mightier in faith united with another.

Jn. 14:12-13, "He that believeth on me, the works that I do shall he do also; and greater works than these shall he do; because I go unto the Father. And whatsoever ye shall ask in my name, that will I do, that the Father may be glorified in the son."

The word "ask" here in the Greek means "to demand."

You are not demanding it of Jesus, but you are demanding it as Peter demanded the man at the beautiful gate to rise and walk.

You are demanding sickness and pain to leave bodies in the Name of Jesus.

He said, "That the Father might be glorified in the Son."

Jn. 15:7: "If ye abide in me, and my words abide in you, ask whatsoever ye will, and it shall be done unto you."

Satan has taken advantage of you. Disease and sickness have made an invalid out of you.

Circumstances have gained the mastery and made a slave instead of a master of you.

Now you abide in Him, and let His Word abide in you.

Let that Word abide in your lips and contend with your sickness and you will become the master again.

You simply insist that that thing is not for you.

You will not stand for defeat any longer.

You can look the adversary in the face and say with quiet assurance, "Satan, you are defeated. In Jesus' Name I demand my rights."

Jn. 16:24: "Hitherto have ye asked nothing in my name: ask, and ye shall receive, that your joy may be made full."

Your joy cannot be made full while loved ones are sick, while men and women are captives of the adversary.

Your joy cannot be made full unless you can see the will of the Father wrought in the lives of men and women around you.

Go, then, and take what belongs to you in that Name.

Hope is the most beautiful child of the senses. The very word is filled with fragrance.

The unthinking have often mistaken it for faith.
Faith is always now.

Hope is always in the future.

Abraham had to change hope into faith.
There is always a battle in the spirit realm to do this.

Hope is so vigorous; it is so full of vibrant enthusiasm.

We thank the Father for it; but it can never be associated with faith, or sit in the seat of faith, or hold dominion over faith.

Faith is the creative element of God.

Hope paints the clouds at the setting of the sun and makes the dying day beautiful.

Faith is a rugged thing, a creative force, a dominating force.

Hope cannot create, and its dominion is oft-times dangerous.

Faith is a builder.

Sense knowledge faith has given us all our great financial structures. It has been the strength of the man of the Senses. It has made him a victor in the war of civilization.

But faith that grows out of the Word, out of the recreated spirit, has given us all that is beautiful and real, all that is holy, all that is actually worthwhile in life.

It has brought us into personal contact with the Creator of the universe.

It has confessed Jesus as Lord.

It has challenged the love heart of the Father resulting in Eternal Life for us: and it has brought man into union with deity.

Chapter The Eleventh

THE FAILURE OF THE HOPER

THIS is one of the most beautiful types of spiritual failures that is known.

So many have mistaken hope for faith. They had a confused idea that if they hoped strong enough they could bring the desired thing to them. They didn't know that hope was future.

There are two scriptures in Romans that will assist us.

Rom. 4:17-18: "(As it is written, a father of many nations have I made thee) before him whom he believed, even God, who giveth life to the dead, and calleth the things that are not, as though they were. Who in hope believed against hope to the end that he might become the father of many nations according to that which had been spoken."

Here was a strange combat: Faith warring with Hope.

Hope wins in most cases, but hope lost here.

Abraham counted the thing for which he had hoped to be his own, and he resolutely put hope aside and claimed the son that God had promised.

But the eighth chapter of Romans, verses twenty-four and twenty-five throw more light upon it: "For in hope were we saved: but hope that is seen is not hope: for who hopeth for that which he seeth? But if we hope for that which we see not then do we with patience wait for it."

Again Heb. 11:1: "Now faith is assurance of things hoped for, a conviction of things not seen."

Here is a different translation: "Faith is the title deed for things hoped for, putting to the proof things not seen." That is the Centenary Translation.

Believing is action. Faith is the cause of the action.

You can see that in this: "Faith is giving substance to things hoped for."

It is bringing into the present tense things which were in the future for us. So we can see that hope is never now.

If I hope for my healing and only have a hope, the undertaker will have a job.

Now a man's investments are all in the future. He bought stocks hoping for a rise. He bought a piece of land hoping that he might sell it in the future to advantage.

Hope has no present-tense blessing. The hoper lives on hopes. The Word is loved, admired, but not acted upon.

The hoper is merely an assenter to the Word. He admires it, knows it is true, will suffer for his convictions of the utter truthfulness of this revelation, but he does not act upon it.

We have many able Bible teachers who are mere hopers or assenters of the Word. Good people, but they have never enjoyed the realities of the things that belong to them. Many of them will act on their creed, but they will not act on the Word.

Often they are assenters to the verbal inspiration. They think all the time that they are believers.

You understand that the believer is a possessor. "He that believeth hath Eternal Life." He that hopes has not yet arrived.

He that hopes may possess sometime, but not now.

The hoper is a present-tense failure as far as the realities of the Word are concerned. He may be a beautiful failure, but he is a failure.

He fails in the midst of rosy hopes. The fragrance of dead hopes fills the air. He fails because he only hopes.

Abraham believed in spite of hope, and brushing hope aside grasped the thing that God had promised.

Many people are in bondage to faith's most dangerous enemy.

Faith is giving substance to that for which we vainly hoped.

Hope has no substance. It is an empty cloud.

Hope deludes the lost; it deludes the sick and the defeated.

There is no hope for the hoper if he remains a hoper.

Prayer that is based on hope is sure to fail.

Salvation that is based on hope never comes to maturity.

The sick person who hopes for healing remains sick.

Let us change hope into faith as Abraham did. Then life will be a success.

Jesus was God speaking. How solemn is that statement. It is pregnant with a challenge from the very throne of God.

He was not only the Word, He was the Living Word. He was the miracle-performing Word. He was the death-destroying Word. He was the life-giving Word.

He said, "I am come that you might have life." That life was the Nature of God, and that Nature of God was in His Words.

When He said in Matt. 24:35 "My words shall never pass away," it was simply a statement of fact.

Just as in 1 Peter 1:23: "Having been begotten again, not of corruptible seed, but of incorruptible, through the Word of God, that liveth and abideth." It lives, and it lives in me, this living "logos," the lifegiving Word of God.

And hear Him whisper, "I watch over this Word to see that it is performed."

Can't you see how safe it is to trust this Living Word?

God speaks; then sets a watch over it to see that it is made good as we trust it or act upon it.

Col. 3:16: "Let the word of Christ dwell in you."

It dwells in you in the measure that you practice it. You may have it committed to memory but if you do not practice it, it doesn't dwell in you.

In Rev. 12:11: "And they overcame him because of the blood of the Lamb, and because of the 'logos' that was in their testimony." That Greek word "logos" is Jesus; and they overcame the devil with Jesus in their lips.

Phil. 4:19: "My God shall supply every need of yours according to his riches in glory in Christ Jesus." That is the "logos" of God in my lips. I stand by it. That is my confession and I maintain it. That is His statement of fact and He stands by it. He meets the need!

1 Peter 2:24: "Who his own self bare our sins in his body upon the tree, that we, having died unto sins, might live unto righteousness; by whose stripes we are healed." That is a little blind to us. Read it like this: "That we having died unto sins might live in the power of His righteousness that has been imparted to us." Then I can act on the Word, "by whose stripes ye were healed."

I know that Word is true. I do not ask Him to heal me, because I am healed. I simply stand by my confession that I am what He says I am.

Stand by your prayers when you have used His Word in your lips. Don't go back on the spoken word from your own lips. You spoke His Word: that was as though He had spoken it.

You said to the Father, "In Jesus' Name I take this"—"I take the salvation of this loved one."

He has given you a legal right to the use of His Name. You hand that Name back to Him with your request.

The Danger of Seeking Experiences

She said, "I know it is true for I experienced it."

It isn't a problem of whether the Word declared it or not. It isn't what the Word says, but what our experience says.

Faith in our experiences is not always faith in the Word. Faith in what I have seen or heard is not always faith in the Word.

Practically all religious experiences are products of the physical senses. It is something felt or heard or seen.

Sense experience always leaves one empty when the experience grows old.

Seeking experiences is always dangerous for it is trusting in the arm of the flesh rather than in the Word, because experiences are always connected with the senses.

Sense experiences are fascinating to a soul-hungry man.

They attract the curious.

They are always in the realm where most folks live.

One of the unfortunate things about seeking experiences is that those who are seeking are in the realm that is governed by evil spirits, for Satan rules most people's bodies, the home of practically all of our experiences.

That is the reason that so many have lost their minds; for when people seek experiences for a long time, demons often take advantage and become their helpers.

They are not wrestling with God. It is not with the Word. They struggle with themselves to get their senses to function.

Sense experiences are always based on sense knowledge faith.

We should remember that sense knowledge always fails us in a crisis; and you will notice that the people who are depending on experiences are ever seeking to have the experience repeated.

They believe in experiences because they live in the realm of the senses.

They never believe the Word. They assent to it, or they hope in it.

Experience-seekers are always unstable in their faith.

The Word of God does not carry as much authority as the word of the person who has the experience.

These people are ever seeking faith.

They have continual war with doubts and fears and discouragements.

They will tell you that they are having a hard battle with the Adversary.

Most of these people have rented a place at the altar.

They are perpetual seekers who long for experiences and power.

They are seeking their healing, not knowing that the Father laid their diseases on Jesus.

They are honest, but they are walking in the realm of the senses.

Their teachers are sense knowledge taught people.

They believe much about the Word, but they do not believe the Word itself.

They act on the word of man and it breaks under them.

They read much about the Bible and about experiences, but they do not study the Word systematically. Consequently they are unstable and double-minded.

They are like people who take dope or liquor. They are drunken with the senses.

If they could only know the sure Word, the unbroken Word, the living Word, the life-giving Word, the all-satisfying Word, they would give up their quest for experiences and let the Word satisfy them.

Seeking Manifestations

What kind of manifestations are they seeking? Something connected with their physical body.

They wish to speak in tongues.

They desire to go under the power.

They wish to have their body vibrate and shake.

They wish to see some physical demonstration of the Spirit's power. The Holy Spirit never gratifies them.

The only spirit that will gratify them is dangerous to play with.

But you ask, "Do you not believe in speaking in tongues?"

Yes, when the Holy Spirit speaks through you it is beautiful.

But no one needs to wait and tarry for Him to do it, for the tarrying gives the Adversary an opportunity to deceive them, and the people who are seeking this are not spiritually minded.

They will not know a demon from the Holy Spirit.

But you say, "Didn't the disciples tarry ten days?"

Yes, they waited until the fulness of time came for the Holy Spirit to come. From that day to this there has been no need to tarry.

The Holy Spirit is here, and He will enter the body of any man or woman who invites Him in.

Luke 11:13: "How much more will your heavenly Father give the Holy Spirit to them that ask him."

You don't receive Eternal Life by tarrying and struggling for it. You receive Eternal Life by acting on the Word.

The same thing is true in regard to the Holy Spirit, and every other blessing that is promised in the Word.

Tarrying means that the Word isn't true and you have to do something to add to its truthfulness, to its veracity.

Waiting before the Lord for power and for some special blessing that you have heard about, is unnecessary because you have in you, if you have received the Holy Spirit, the fountain of all experiences.

You have invited the Holy Spirit to make His home in your body; and He said if you did, He would come in and occupy it.

Well, you have only one thing to do: that is to accept that statement of His as absolutely true, and thank Him—feeling or no feeling—that He has come into your body to make His home.

Now you allow Him to take over your life.

You are not passive, but you are insistent that He take you over; that He illumine your heart and your mind, that He will now guide you into all the reality of the redemptive work of Christ that belongs to you; that He prove Himself to be greater in you than the forces of darkness that are around you.

He is the power of God, the mind of God, the ability of God, and He is in you.

But give Him place, honor Him, treat Him with the utmost courtesy.

Become accustomed to talking with Him; He is your continual companion.

He is to guide you daily.

After a while you will be able to say, "Is it right to do this?" and you will get a "yes" or a "no" in your spirit.

When you have a few minutes to study the Word, remember He is there. He will illumine it.

As you meditate, He will unveil to you the deeper, hidden meanings in the Word that are necessary in your spiritual life, or to those to whom you are ministering.

Act as though He were there.

Plan your work with a consciousness that greater is He that is in you than he that is in the world.

He is the one that can make Jesus wisdom unto you through the Word.

He can make the Word a living thing in your lips.

He gives you ability to use the Name so that all the authority that is in that Name can be exercised by you.

Experiences are not spiritual realities always, but the Holy Spirit's presence in you unveiling the Word, brings into your spirit consciousness realities of the highest value.

We Must Not Fail Him

He has committed unto us the word of Grace.
He has committed unto us the Word of Wisdom.
He has committed unto us His ability.

Have you ever taken notice of what you are in Christ? Of what you have, and of what you can do?

Why, you are the very sons and daughters of God Almighty. You have His life and nature in you.

You have the great mighty Holy Spirit who raised Jesus from the dead.

What can you do?

Measure it by the ability of God that is at work within you. Measure it by His own wonderful Word.

He knew what needs would face us when He was planning our Redemption and when He was planning the New Creation. I can hear Him say: "I'll identify myself with them; I'll be in them; I'll work through them. My ability shall become their ability, my wisdom their wisdom. I won't let them fail. Through the Word I will build myself into them."

Underestimating the work that God wrought in Christ is the sin of ignorance.

Most of us are guilty of it.

The Pauline Revelation has never become a part of our spiritual education. Most sermon texts come from the Old Testament or from the four gospels.

For that reason we have underestimated the work He did for us.

We have underestimated the work that He did in us, in the New Creation.

And of course, we underestimate what He can do through us.

The secret of dominating faith lies in getting a true conception of what Jesus actually did for us, and what we are in Him as a result of it, and what the Word promises we can do as a result of His finished work in us.

Knowledge that is not acted upon is of no value.

You know what Jesus did for you in His Substitution; then you dare to act on that knowledge.

That is the highest order of faith.

Simply to admire it, to say that you believe it, but to refuse to act upon it, robs you of faith in the time of need.

When I know what He is and what He did for me, what actually belongs to me now, and what I may enjoy in my daily life, it makes me a victor.

When I know that Eph. 1:3 is real, that "he has blessed me with every spiritual blessing in Christ Jesus," and I know how to assimilate that, how to enjoy it, how to enter into the riches of it, then I appreciate my Master.

I am getting to know Him.

I am getting to the place in my spiritual growth where I begin to recognize the riches of His grace, and the riches of His finished work, and the riches of His own nature that has been imparted to me.

Chapter The Twelfth

UNDERESTIMATING JESUS

NE cannot conceive of anything that will cripple faith and put the believer in bondage more quickly and surely than underestimating what He is, and what we are in Him. Along with that will come an underestimation of the Word.

We will say right out, "Oh, I believe the Bible is the Word of God." And yet we turn to the arm of flesh for help.

And when we pray, we do not come with that quiet assurance that we would if some banker had given us his word in regard to our financial standing at the bank.

This is an unconscious underestimation of the Word, and it is an unconscious underestimation of the integrity of the Master Himself, who is the Author of this Word.

This leads to weakness, to doubt and fear.

It makes a vacillating type of faith.

We become what James calls "a double-minded man that is unstable in all his ways."

What will change it?

When we realize what He has done for us in His great Substitution and in the New Creation.

We should meditate on the fact that we are partakers of the divine nature. "These things have I written unto you, that ye may know that ye have Eternal Life, even to you that believe on His name." 1 John 5:13.

If we say over and over again to our hearts: "I am a partaker of God's very nature. I have in me His faith nature. This makes me a child of faith. I have been begotten of the Living Word through the Holy Spirit. The real me was recreated in Christ. I have the very nature of the Father and the Father is love, so I have in me the love nature of the Father," if we meditate on this, we will no longer be "double-minded men."

Repeat it over and over again.

Hold it as a constant affirmation before your mind that you are what He says you are; that you are a partaker of His very nature as He has declared.

And you remember that "greater is He that is in you, than he that is in the world." That Greater One is the Holy Spirit.

The Holy Spirit is the one that in creation gave the color, the beauty and fragrance to the flowers, to vegetation, to the trees. He is the one that takes of the nature of the Father, and through the Word, builds it into us.

He builds the beauty of Christ into our conduct.

He touches our reasoning faculties until the things that He has made in the floral world assume a new interest, and their beauty is enhanced and their fragrance enjoyed as never before.

I can remember the night that I received Eternal Life. It seemed as though I hardly touched the sidewalk on my way home. It was a cold winter night in January, but, oh, how beautiful the snow and the frost. Yes, the trees stripped of their foliage assumed a beauty I had never noted before.

The Holy Spirit had taken possession and was unveiling the wonders of His grace to me.

An underestimation of the Holy Spirit, of the Word, of Jesus, will keep us in a state of flux, in a realm of uncertainty.

Fear will dominate us; doubt will bind us, and hold us in the realm of weakness.

But when we come to know Jesus as our Lord, as the Mighty One at the right hand of the Father who ever lives to make intercession for us, our great lawyer that looks after every legal need of ours in Christ, we will no longer be dominated by fear and doubt.

We should come to know the reality of the Holy Spirit's reality, which is all unveiled to us in the Pauline Revelation.

I urge you to go back and read Romans, and First and Second Corinthians again. Then abide a while in Ephesians, in those first three chapters especially, until you are lifted out of the realm of the senses into the realm of the new man in Christ Jesus.

What He Made Us

The fear of seeing what we are in Christ, and of acting as though we knew what we were, has kept us in bondage and robbed us of the reality of His finished work. How slow we have been to act what we are in Him. The Spirit, through the Word, has declared what we are in Christ. Eph. 1:7 "in whom we have our redemption through his blood, the remission of our trespasses"—and it is according to the riches of His Grace.

That is not a theological redemption. This is not Paul's philosophy. This is the Father's description of what we are in His Son, and He says "in whom we have our redemption."

From Whom and What are we redeemed?

Satan is the God of Darkness. We have been delivered out of Satan's Dominion, out of the realm and authority of Darkness. We have been delivered out of the dominion of Sin, for "Sin shall not have dominion over you." We are delivered out of the authority of Disease, for Rom. 8:11 says: "If the Spirit of him that raised up Jesus from the dead dwelleth in you, he that raised up Christ Jesus from the dead shall give life also to your mortal bodies through his Spirit that dwelleth in you."

Not only have we a redemption that is literal and absolute, but we are a new creation, and Satan has no dominion over us.

Jesus is the Head and Lord of this new creation.

We have been taught so long and so persistently about our weaknesses and our lack of ability and our unworthiness that we hardly dare say that we are what He says we are. We are afraid that people will misunderstand us and think that we have become fanatical.

But He says: "Wherefore if any man is in Christ (and we are in Christ) he is a new creation: the old things are passed away; behold, they are become new, and all these things are of God," and we are reconciled to Him.

We are a part of His very dream.

Satan has no dominion over this new creation.

Eph. 2:10 says we are created in Christ Jesus, that when Jesus arose from the dead the work of the new creation was consumated in Christ. It became a reality in us when we took Him as our Savior and confessed Him as our Lord.

The Father in His Word has declared what we are in His Son. That declaration is the truth.

I may not have grown up to it, may not have appreciated it, but it stands there with an open door inviting me to enjoy all the fulness that is mine in Him.

He declares what we may do in the name of His Son. We haven't appreciated it perhaps, but He gave to us the power of attorney to use His Son's name.

Jesus said, "Hitherto ye have asked nothing in my name; ask and receive that your joy may be made full."

Seven times Jesus repeats this, giving us the legal right to the use of His name.

Phil. 2:9-10 tells us that this name is above every name, and at the name of Jesus every knee should bow, beings in Heaven, beings on earth, and beings under the earth, and every tongue shall confess that Jesus is Lord to the glory of God my Father.

Not only that, but Jesus said after He arose from the dead, "All authority hath been given unto me in heaven and on earth.

Go ye therefore, and make disciples of all the nations." Disciple means a student, a learner. He never said, "Go and make converts;" he never said, "Go and make churches," but "Go and make disciples."

There will be schools of Christ. Every believer will be a student of this living Word. What Masters they will be!

Not only do we have that power to use the name of Jesus to cast out demons, or to heal the sick, but that Name gives us access to the Father, and is the absolute guarantee of answered prayer.

You see, this prayer life is based upon absolute knowledge.

It is not based upon emotion nor feelings nor the theories of men, but upon the Living Word of God, this Word that "Liveth and Abideth."

When you know in your heart that you are what He says you are, then you act it in the face of all, confessing what He has done in you, confessing what He has made you. This glorifies Him and His Work.

To deny what we are, to tell what Satan is doing in our bodies and minds, is denying what we are in Christ.

When Jesus said, "All things are possible to him that believeth," He meant that all things are possible to the Believer. All that Believer needs to do is to get to know what he is in Christ, then rise up and take his place.

What Masters He has made us to be! How invincible we are!

Can't you see what it would mean for one in the face of all this to be talking about his weakness, his lack, making his confession of his inability.

"Of His fulness have we all received," and it is grace and the ability of God for us to enjoy to the very limit all that we are in Him.

Jesus

The Man at the right hand of God, who loved me and died for me, now ever lives for me!

He was God's answer to the universal cry of humanity.

He was God manifest to our senses.

He was an intrusion into the sense realm.

He talked like God. He acted like God. He lived like God, and and on the cross He died like God.

He was not a philosopher searching for the truth. He was the truth.

He was not a mystic. He was reality.

He was not an experimenter searching for reality.

He was not a reformer. He was the Recreator.

He was not a visionary. He was the Light of the world.
He never reflected.
He never reasoned.
He knew. He never learned.
He never asked prayers for Himself.
He never sought the help of man.
He was never in a hurry.
He was never afraid.
He never showed weakness.
He never hesitated.
He was always ready.
He was sure. There was a sureness in all He did or said.
He had no sense of sin or need of forgiveness.
He never sought or needed advice.
He knew why He came.
He knew from whence He came.
He knew who He was.
He knew the Father.
He knew about heaven.
He knew where He was going.
He knew man.
He knew Satan.
He had no sense of lack.
He had no sense of limitations.

From the Arrest To the Cross

He had no sense of fear.
He had no anger, no sense of dissappointment, no sense of being defeated or being forsaken.
He had no sense of need of human sympathy.
He didn't shrink from pain or brutal treatment.
He was master when they arrested Him.
He was the master at the trial.
He ruled the seen and the unseen while He was on the cross.
He was Almighty, yet a man.
He died as God.

After the Resurrection

He had no sense of revenge. He was love.
He was a revelation of a new kind of love.
There were no dramatics. He said, "Go tell Peter, the weakest one."
He died a Lamb. He arose as Lord.
He acted like God.

He spoke like God.
His resurrection had all the simplicity of God.
He was God.

His Word Is Spirit and Life

Jesus knew the value and authority of His own words, and He dared to say, "The words that I speak unto you, they are spirit and they are life."

He knew that His words were living things.

He knew that His words would give life and death.

You remember how He spoke to the barren fig tree and it died from the root up.

You know that He spoke to the widow's son, and he became alive instantly.

When the Holy Spirit speaks through Paul, Heb. 4:12: "The 'logos' of God is a living thing," the Spirit is simply repeating in different words what Jesus said: "The words that I speak are spirit and they are life."

James 1:18 says we are begotten by the Word, the Word that recreates men and gives them life.

1 Pet. 1:23 holds a peculiar place in the heart of deeply spiritual men: "Having been begotten again, not of corruptible seed, but of incorruptible, through the word of God, which liveth and abideth."

Our birth into the spiritual realm, the thing that gave us eternal life and made us a branch of the vine, was the incorruptible Word of God.

Psalms 107:20: "He sent His word and healed them."

That word was His Son.

That word we know by the Name of Jesus: "In the beginning was the word, and the word was with God, and the word was God."

That is the Word that brought Eternal Life to us.

Paul, saying goodbye to the Ephesian brethren, says in Acts. 20:32: "Now I commend you to God, and to the word of his grace, which is able to build you up, and give you the inheritance among all them that are sanctified."

This Word is the faith-building Word, the grace-revealing Word, the Word of assurance.

This Word Is Our Testimony

Rom. 10:8: "The word of faith, which we preach."

John 8:31-32: "If ye abide in my word, then are ye truly my

disciples; and you shall know the truth, and the truth shall make you free."

We abide in the Word.

We live in it.

Our home is in the Word.

But John 15:7 takes a step beyond: "If ye abide in me, and my words abide in you, you shall demand your rights, and they will come into being for you." (Lit. Trans.)

The thought of the Greek is like something born, "Coming into being;" and so He says the thing that you desire, if His words abide in you, will be given birth by God.

It is a staggering thing, isn't it?

There is absolutely no limit to the ability of God that is unveiled to us in His Word.

The Word Of God

The Word is of God, outbreathings of God, the mind of God, the will of God.

It is God speaking.

It is a part of God Himself. It is a living thing.

It abides forever.

"I watch over my word."

"No word from God is void of power."

God and His Word are One.

This Word can live in my heart.

I will obey it—I will do it—I will enjoy it!

Faith In the Written Word

All the mighty achievements wrought by men of God have been accomplished by faith in the written Word.

It was the Word made flesh. Jesus spoke the Word. He was the Word.

Now it is my faith in the Living Word, the written Word.

It is that Word in my lips that heals the sick, that breaks the power of demons over men.

I hold it in my hand.

I have it in my heart.

I have it in my lips.

I live it.

It lives in me.

The Word is my healing, my strength.

It is the bread of life to me.

It is the strength, the very ability of God to me.

The Word is my confession.

The Word is my light and my salvation.

The Word is my rest, my pillow.

The Word gives me quietness in the midst of confusion; gives me victory in the midst of defeat.

It gives me joy where desolation reigned.

The Word in my lips becomes the living, life-saving, soul-inspiring voice of God.

I Know What God's Word In My Lips Will Do

First, it is the Word in your heart; then it is the Word in your lips.

Jesus knew what His Father's Word would do in His lips.

Peter and John knew what the Word would do in their lips.

It is the Word that goeth forth out of my mouth, that cannot return unto Him void.

The creative Word in the lips of Jesus is the creative Word in your lips.

Faith, is daring to speak His Word to the sick, to the demon-possessed and setting them free.

Real prayer is taking His Word into the Throne Room and letting His Word speak through your lips to Him on the Throne, calling His attention to His own promises.

The written Word is God's testimony about Himself, about His Son and about His Family.

It is also a testimony about His old enemy that has sought to destroy the object of His affection, man.

Some Word Facts

The Gospel of John is largely Jesus' testimony about Himself and about His Father.

It is a remarkable fact that Exodus, Leviticus, Numbers, and Deuteronomy are the testimony of Jehovah. About 2500 times, He says, "I am Jehovah."

We have never given place in our thinking to the importance of the right confession.

The Word is God speaking to me.

It is a Revelation to me.

So many of us wish to demonstrate our faith; that is, to prove to our own heart's satisfaction our own confidence in the Word.

Here is the relation of Confession to Demonstration. Rom. 10:9-10 says: "Because if thou shalt confess with thy mouth Jesus as Lord, and believe in thy heart that God raised him from the dead, thou shalt be saved: for with the heart man believeth unto righteousness; and with the lips confession is made unto salvation."

Notice that confession precedes possession.

You do not have Eternal Life until you confess the Lordship of Jesus and your confidence in His substitutionary sacrifice.

John 6:47: "He that believeth hath Eternal Life."

There is no possession without action. Believing is acting on the Word.

Acting on the Word is your confession.

Let it be a fixed fact in your mind that confession is proof of faith.

There is no believing that does not climax in confession.

It is faith expressing itself.

So believing and confessing are practically one.

Your confession locates you. I know where you are. I know what you are.

Mental assent dares not confess.

It wishes to be sure of results first, so it always stands on the negative side of the issue.

It never wins.

It is never a success.

Mental assent is the voice of the senses, the mind of the senses, or the mind of the flesh.

Faith is from the mind of the spirit—your recreated spirit, dominating your reason faculties.

The mind of the senses is a spiritually dead mind.

1 Cor. 2:14 says: "Now the natural (or physical) man understands not the things of the Spirit of God: for they are foolishness unto him."

There is only one attitude to take toward the spiritually dead or the mentally blinded one. They cannot enjoy the riches that belong to them until they act intelligently upon the Word.

Let me state it from another angle: The natural man cannot understand or appreciate the things of God however hungry he may be for them, but he may recognize the need of them, so God has placed these riches within his reach.

All he needs to do is act upon the Word, and they become his.

Treating the Word As If It Were a Common Book

One of the most dangerous habits that Christians have is treating the Word as though it were a common book.

In one breath we will declare that we believe it to be a Revelation from God, and yet we turn to the arm of flesh for help when the Word has promised perfect deliverance.

We treat the fact of Redemption as though it were a beautiful fiction.

We read articles about the Word.

We sing hymns confessing it.

And yet we live under the dominion of the Adversary, continually confessing sickness, want, fear, weakness, and doubts in the face of this Revelation from God of our Redemption, of the substitutionary sacrifice of Christ, and the fact that He is seated now at the right hand of God having finished a work that perfectly satisfys the demands of Justice and meet the needs of humanity.

We read about it. We talk about it.

And then we act as though it were but a fable!

This is the reason why the church has more sickness and disease than any other organized body of people; why faith is weak; why the average believer is ruled by the Adversary.

All this could be changed if we would give the Word the same place we would give Christ if He were here physically in our presence.

Our Words

We are in our words.

They are born in us.

They are part of us.

We live in them.

They live in others.

We know each other by our words.

Our words are ourselves.

Words are given to express ourselves.

The Bible is born of God. He gave birth to it. He gave life to His own Word.

He is in it.

It is a part of Him.

We know God by His Word.

He has expressed Himself in it.

God lives in His Word in our lips.

This sets Jesus free to heal, save, and bless.

Jesus is the Word—He lives in the Word.

The Word lives in us.

The Word's Lordship is over us.

We know the Father through the Word.

We know Jesus by His Words.

Some have said that prayer is the greatest opportunity ever offered to a man in Christ.

If this is true then you can understand why there would be enemies to stand in the way of a prayer life.

You can understand why the Adversary would make it his business to see that the prayer life of an individual, and of a church, should be ineffective.

Satan would not be a good General, he would not be a Strategist unless the prayer life should be destroyed.

A church is as powerful as its prayer life.

The men and women who learn the secret of reaching the throne, getting the ear of God, become dangerous to the hosts of darkness.

John Knox stood alone when he fought Bloody Mary. She feared him more than she feared the combined armies of the world.

Martin Luther's prayers gave birth to the Reformation.

His knowledge and experience of the New Birth would not have given birth to that mighty upheaval in Germany unless that man had had a prayer life.

When John Knox cried, "Give me Scotland or I die;" and when Martin Luther said, "I will not let go of you, God, until you give me Germany," God heard them.

And He is as easily reached now as He ever was. It is not a problem of education, but of knowing your rights and privileges, and then daring to enter the throne room facing God with the needs of the world.

Chapter The Thirteenth

SOME ENEMIES OF PRAYER

SOME of these Enemies are very dear friends. We have associated with them for many years, and it will be hard for us to give them up.

One of them is a desire to read about the Bible and about Prayer rather than to study the Word and fit ourselves for this, the highest and holiest of all vocations.

More than a vocation, it is a privilege, the rarest of all privileges that have been given to us in Grace.

I am convinced that the most outstanding Enemy is a lack of knowledge of what we are in Christ, and of what He is in us, what He did for us, and of our standing and legal rights before the throne.

This language is to many strange, but I want you to come to know what actually belongs to you in Christ.

Until you do, you will never have a prayer life beyond the baby experience.

In another chapter we are taking up what we are in Christ, what our privileges and abilities are, but now I want you to think of these Enemies that stand in the way of our really assuming our responsibilities.

Another Enemy is ignorance of what "Believing" is.

You remember that the word "believe" is a verb. It is an action word—it means to act upon the Word.

Then believing the Word is simply acting on it, as we act upon the word of our government in regard to taxes, or of our banker in regard to our overdrawn account.

When Jesus says, "If ye abide in me, and my words abide in you, ye shall ask what ye will and it shall be done unto you," you simply act on that word.

There is no believing without acting, and believing means having possession.

I possess what the Word has promised me.

For instance, here is a statement of fact: "Surely He hath born my sicknesses and carried my pains and I have come to esteem Him as the one stricken, smitten of God, and afflicted." (Lit.)

I don't try to believe this—I merely act upon it.

I say, "Did God say that He laid my diseases on Jesus and that God afflicted Him with them? Well, then if He did, by His stripes I am healed."

I don't try to believe it, because it is true. God said it, and what God says is!

What do I do? I look up and say, "Father, I thank you that at last I have found the truth—I am healed. I am so happy that at last this great fact has been unveiled to me in your Word."

Don't try to believe. Don't condemn yourself because you do not believe, but learn to act on His Word as you act on the word of anyone else.

If you went to a doctor and he prescribed for you, you would take the prescription to the druggist and act on it, wouldn't you? Do the same thing with His Word.

Wrong Confession

Another desperate Enemy, and a persistent one, is Wrong Confession.

What do I mean by Wrong Confession?

You know that Christianity is really the Great Confession. Rom. 10:9. "Because if thou shalt confess with thy mouth Jesus as Lord, and shalt believe in thy heart that God raised him from the dead, thou shalt be saved."

You notice it is a confession here with your lips.

(Whenever the word "Confession" is used we unconsciously think of sin. It is not confession of sin. It is a confession of our knowing that God's Son died for our sins according to Scripture, and that the third day He was raised again.)

Now, with my mouth I make confession of the Lordship of that raised One. I not only do that, but with my heart I have accepted His Righteousness and I make confession of my Salvation.

You see there is no such thing as salvation without Confession.

So Heb. 3:1 becomes clear: "Wherefore, holy brethren, partakers of a heavenly calling, consider the Apostle and High Priest of our confession, even Jesus."

You see, Christianity is our Confession.

Heb. 4:14 He says, "Let us hold fast our confession."

What is our Confession? Why, that God is our Father, we are His Children, we are in His Family.

It is a Confession that our Father knows what our needs are and has made provision to meet everyone of them.

It is a Confession of the finished work of Christ, of what I am in Him, and what He is in me.

It is a Confession that "greater is He that is in me, than he that is in the world."

It is my Confession that my God does supply every need of mine according to His riches in glory.

It is my Confession that when I pray, the Father hears my prayer and answers me.

This is a manifold Confession.

If I were sick, I would maintain my Confession that "by His stripes I am healed."

If I were weak, I would insist upon this Confession that God is now "the strength of my life," and I can do all things in Him who is enabling me with His own ability.

If it is a problem of wisdom, I Confess that Jesus has been made unto me Wisdom from God.

Hope

Another Enemy is Hope.

Hope is always future. Faith is always now.

Someone comes to me and asks me to pray for them, and I say, "Was the prayer answered?" And they answer, "I hope it was."

Then I know it will not be answered, and I frankly tell them. "No, the Hoper's prayers are seldom answered."

Hope is a beautiful thing when it is about Heaven, or the coming back of the Master, and everything that belongs to the future. But for present-tense practices and present-tense life, hope is a dangerous enemy.

It is beautiful, but it is dangerous!

The Hoper is always a failure. It is the Believer that is a success—and believing, you remember, is acting on the Word.

Mental Assent   *James 1:22-25*

Another Enemy is Mental Assent.

You say, "What is it?" It is mentally accepting the Word as true, but not acting upon it.

It is admiring the Word.

You may have been called a Fundamentalist, and you may have confessed that you believe the Word from Genesis to Revelation; but when it comes to acting on it, you have never done it.

You are like one that knows all the ingredients that are in a certain dish that you have for dinner.

You are able to diagnose every feature about it. But you don't eat it. It does you no good.

The Mental Assenter is a failure, a beautiful failure, but a failure.

I say, "Is that Word true?" And you declare, "It is true. I believe every word from Genesis to Revelation." You are self-deceived.

The Believer is a "doer of the Word and not a hearer only."

Jesus described him in that last illustration of the Sermon on the Mount. The Doer was the one who dug deep, went down to the rock and built his house thereon. The Mental Assenter built on the sand. Matthew 7:24-27

Praying for Faith

Another Enemy is Praying for Faith.

How many times we have gone to the altar and to the prayer room to pray for more faith. What a delusion it was.

You never heard of anyone getting more faith or having their faith increased by praying for it.

Why? Because the prayer for faith is a prayer based on unbelief.

If unbelief were not your master, you wouldn't need faith; so praying for faith is an absolute proof that you will not get it, and that you are insulting the Father by doing it.

Why, if a child should say to its mother, "Mama, I want you to increase my faith in you. I've been trying all morning to believe that what you said about that trip this Saturday was true." The child is insulting the integrity of his mother.

So when you pray for faith you are insulting the author of the Word. You don't intend to, but you are doing that.

Depending on Another's Faith

Another Enemy of prayer is our dependence on other people's faith.

We become unconsciously, spiritual hitchhikers.

To every man God has given a measure of Faith; that Faith came with the New Creation, it came when you received the Father's Nature. That Nature is a Faith Nature.

As soon as it came into you and you became His Child, you began to develop that Faith.

Just as you develop your mental strength by certain mental exercises, and develop your physical strength by certain physical exercises, now you are developing your faith by feeding on the Word. (John 15:7)

You begin to live in the Word.

You are acting on the Word.

You are taking advantage of your privileges in Christ.

Here Are Some Don'ts

Don't try to believe, just act on the Word.

Don't have a double confession so that one moment you confess, "Yes, He heard my prayer. I am healed," or "I will get the money," and then begin to question how it is going to come and what you ought to do to get it.

Your latter confession destroys the first.

A wrong confession destroys prayer and destroys faith.

Don't trust in other people's faith—have your own.

Do your own believing. Have your own faith as you have your own clothes. Act on the Word for yourself.

Don't talk doubt or unbelief.

Never admit that you are a "Doubting Thomas;" that is an insult to your Father.

Don't talk about sickness and disease.

Never talk about failure. Talk about the Word, its absolute integrity, and of your utter confidence in it; of your ability to act on it; and hold fast to your confession of its truthfulness.

"Why call ye me Lord, Lord?" Jesus is describing the man who talks very religiously but does not do the Word.

You cannot build Faith without practicing the Word.

You cannot develop a Prayer Life that is anything but words unless the Word actually has a part in your life.

You live the Word; you do the Word.

One may be a teacher of the Bible. He may know the Book from Genesis to Revelation, but he does not walk by Faith. He lives in the realm of the Senses.

James describes him very minutely. James 1:22-25: "But be ye doers of the word, and not hearers only, deluding your own selves."

There is a vast army of self-deluders today. They teach the Word, they talk the Word, they preach the Word, but they do not practice it.

The measure that I live the Word is the measure of my Faith.

My Prayer Life is valuable only in the measure that the Word in my lips is a living thing. It lives only as I practice it.

"If one is a hearer of the Word and not a doer, he is like a man beholding his natural face in a mirror and he goes away and straightway forgets what manner of man he is."

What manner of man is he?

Why, he is the new man in Christ.

He is the new creation man.

He is a member of the body of Christ.

He is a son with a legal standing and the ability of God, and yet he lives like a common man.

He has a standing invitation to visit in the throne room any time that he wishes.

He has the righteousness of God which enables him to stand in the Father's presence with the same freedom that Jesus possessed.

But he lives like a common man, and when a crisis comes he is hunting for someone to believe for him.

True, he can pray. He is quite adept at that, but his prayers are but empty words when he might have them filled with Faith, born of a real fellowship with the Father.

He is a hearer that "forgetteth," a believer that is not a doer, a professor without living and walking in the Word.

It is a wonderful thing to be a doer of Jesus' Words. This is the real secret of a prayer life.

I don't know whether it has ever been a reality in your life or not that you are a love creation and, therefore, a Lover by Nature because you are a possessor of the Father's Nature.

You should do identically as Jesus did.

He did the Father's Will.

He lived the Father's Will.

He spoke the Father's Words.

He was a doer as well as a hearer and because He was that, the believer has a right to call Jesus "Lord" and expect that Jesus will fulfill a Lord's part to him in his daily walk.

Now I can quietly say, "The Lord is my shepherd and I do not want" for He and I walk together.

Confusing the Prayer Problem

Those who have depended upon prayer as a means of carrying on their religious activities have oft-times been driven to extremeties because the money didn't come, or some other problem that confronted them could not seem to be solved; and so they have resorted to using methods and means suggested by others.

The lives of many men of prayer have been a strong incentive to a life of Faith on the part of many, and their method of prayer has influenced these earnest hearts greatly.

In my early days after I had given up my income and started to live what we call a "life of faith," these problems confronted me.

I heard about "battle prayer" and we tried it. We stormed the throne. We cried aloud; but somehow or other it didn't bring the results, and I wondered why.

Then we heard about "praying through," and we tried that

We prayed through our problems.

After a while I discovered that it was all works on my part and the part of those whose footsteps I had followed; that "holding onto God" until the answer came, or "praying hard," were expressions which came from the realm of the senses.

It was sense knowledge trying to solve a faith problem, a spiritual problem.

Then suddenly it occurred to me that we hadn't been acting on the Word.

Instead we had read the Word, and then tried to force God to do something.

We had forgotten that "No word from God is void of power," and "I watch over my Word to perform it."

We had forgotten John 15:7: "If ye abide in me, and my words abide in you, ye shall ask whatsoever ye will, and it shall be given unto you."

The Name of Jesus had not yet functioned, and we didn't know John 15:16: "Whatsoever ye ask of the Father in my name, he will give it you;" or John 16:23-24.

I had never fathomed the secret of the Master's teaching about His Name.

Now it began to dawn on me. We had prayed to Jesus. We had prayed to the Holy Spirit. We had prayed to God.

Now we came to the place where we saw we should pray to the Father in Jesus' Name.

We saw that we are to take the Master's place, and the Master had given us the power of attorney to use His Name. (Read, "The Wonderful Name")

That dawned on our spirit.

It changed our whole attitude about prayer.

John 16:26-27: "In that day ye shall ask in my name: and I say not unto you, that I will pray the Father for you; for the Father himself loveth you, because ye have loved me, and have believed that I came forth from the Father."

This brings us into intimate contact with the Father in Jesus Name.

Verses 23 and 24 are now clear: "In that day ye will not pray to me. Verily, verily, I say unto you, If ye shall ask anything of the Father, he will give it you in my name. Hitherto have ye asked nothing in my name. Ask, and ye shall receive, that your joy may be made full."

Then prayer is based upon the simple ground of coming to the Father in Jesus' Name.

His love outreaching toward us caused Him to go a step be-

yond that, and in Heb. 4:16, He invites us to come boldly to the
throne of grace.

The Greek word "grace" means "love gifts."

Then the throne room is a room where love gifts are given
lavishly to those who love Him.

So I am invited to come boldly, fearlessly, as a son in the
Father's presence, or as a love-slave of Jesus, into His presence.

You see, there is no "battle prayer" there. There is no "praying through."

I am there in His presence to make my needs known.

Praying According To His Will

In praying, the problem came up about prayer being according
to the will of the Father.

I made this sweet discovery: that I had taken Jesus' place
here on the earth, and that I was carrying out the plan of Redemption in bringing lost men to the saving knowledge of Christ, building up the babes in Christ, setting the captives free, healing the
sick, doing the same kind of work that the Master did in His
earth walk.

Then He comforted me greatly by giving me 1 John 5:14-15:
"This is the boldness which we have toward him, (I like another
rendering: "This is the freedom that we have in his presence,")
that, if we ask anything according to his will, he heareth us: and if
we know that he heareth us whatsoever we ask, we know that we
have the petitions which we have asked of him."

We know that Jesus was the Will of the Father manifest.
He said, "I came not to do mine own will, but the will of him that
sent me."

He climaxed it by saying: "I always do the things that are
pleasing to my Father." (John 8:29.)

Then if we do the same things that Jesus did, plus the things
that He has taught us to do that He could not do, we may be sure
that we are in the Father's will.

And if we are in His will, then we are certain that our prayers
are answered.

We don't try to force Him to answer them.

We don't tease Him like some children do their parents until
they wear their parents out.

No. We come as intelligent men and women, grown up in
Christ, and take our place, bearing His burdens, fellowshipping
His purposes in saving the world.

We come into the throne room, that room of love gifts, into
the very presence of the Father, and we talk things over with Him.

But you say, "Don't you think sometimes it is necessary to pray all night? Jesus did."

If we knew the nature of Jesus' prayers during those night sessions that might help us.

If you have needs enough that it would take a whole night to cover them, then you should take the night.

"Don't you think that we should keep on praying until our prayer is answered?"

No. I think instead we might remind Him and thank Him for it.

Unbelief becomes insistent, thinking that by works of some kind it can force God to answer.

We are going to act on His Word just as we act on the word of any firm or company. We are going to act on His Word simply as intelligent men and women act on the word of a bank or any other institution that has a record of honesty.

Remember, God cannot lie. He watches over His Word to make it good.

The man that trusts Him is absolutely as safe as Jesus was when He trusted His Father.

A Little Study About the Defeated One

When Jesus began His public ministry He came in contact instantly with demoniacal forces.

They had wrought unhindered through all the ages. They had held men in bondage. They reigned as kings in the realm of spiritual death.

No one had authority to dispossess them or to rule over them.

Mark 1:21-24: "And they go into Capernaum; and straightway on the sabbath day he entered into the synagogue and taught. And they were astonished at his teaching: for he taught them as having authority, and not as the scribes. And straightway there was in their synagogue a man with an unclean spirit; and he cried out, saying, What have we to do with thee, thou Jesus of Nazareth? Art thou come to destroy us? I know thee who thou art, the Holy One of God."

That demon knew Jesus, knew who He was.

He not only knew Jesus, but he knew His authority and His attitude toward him.

Demons feared Him.

Luke 4:1-13 is the story of the temptation of Jesus. Jesus proved Himself to be the master of Satan, and the demons must have known of Satan's defeat.

They recognized their master.

Heb. 2:14: "Since then the children are sharers in flesh and blood, he also himself in like manner partook of the same; that through death he might bring to nought, (or paralyze) the death-dealing power of Satan."

Rev. 1:17-18: "And when I saw him, I fell at his feet as one dead. And he laid his right hand upon me, saying, Fear not, I am the First and the Last, and the Living one; and I was dead, and behold, I am alive for evermore, and I have the keys of death and of Hades."

Jesus conquered Satan as we are shown in Col. 2:15: "Having put off from himself the principalities and the powers, he made a show of them openly, triumphing over them in it." This is Satan's eternal defeat.

You can understand Heb. 9:12: "Nor yet with the blood of goats and calves, but with his own blood, entered in once for all into the holy place, having obtained eternal redemption." (Lit.)

During Jesus' earth walk He defeated Satan at every point of contact, from the day of His temptation until He surrendered Himself on the cross.

1 Cor. 2:6 Moffatt translates: "We speak wisdom, however, among them that are fullgrown; not a wisdom of the dethroned powers that rule this world."

Satan and the demoniacal forces are dethroned.

In Col. 2:15 I showed you that they were disarmed and stripped of their authority; and in Heb. 2:14 Jesus destroyed the authority of the Lord of death.

Rom. 5:17—Weymouth's Trans.: "For if, by the trespass of the one, death seized the sovereignty through that one; much more shall they that receive the abundance of grace and the gift of righteousness reign as kings in the realm of life."

The New Creation, who was the defeated one, the conquered one, now reigns as a king in the realm of life here among men, where he had served as a slave of spiritual death.

Eph. 1:22-23: "And he put all things in subjection under his feet, and gave him to be head over all things for the benefit of the church, which is his body, the fulness of him that filleth all in all."

2 Cor. 2:14 is the Spirit's paean of praise of victory over Satanic forces. Let me give it to you from Conybeare: "But thanks be to God who leads me on from place to place in the train of his triumph, to celebrate his victory over the enemies of Christ, (those enemies are not men, they are demons.) and by me sends forth the knowledge of Him, a stream of fragrant incense, throughout the

world. For Christ's is the fragrance which I offer up to God."
(Literally, "Christ's fragrance am I unto God.")

Now in the face of these facts, what should be our attitude toward the Adversary and his works?

You remember in 1 John 3:8: "To this end was the Son of God manifested that he might destroy the works of the devil."

We are taking Jesus' place.

We are acting for Him.

He was a destroyer of the works of the Adversary: we should follow in His steps.

Paul, though a prisoner in Rome, said, "I, Paul, the prisoner of Jesus Christ."

He was not a prisoner of circumstances, nor of men, nor of government. They might hold him in captivity, but he knew that if it was the Father's will for him to be set free, he would be set free as he was in Philippi.

He was not the prisoner of Rome. He was the prisoner of Jesus Christ.

The revelation that God gave to Paul finally destroyed the Roman Empire. It destroys everything that opposes the will and mind of the Father where it is unveiled, where men understand it. Where believers enter into its fulness, they become masters.

What should be our attitude today?

Should we cowardly yield to the forces of darkness?

Should we submit to Satanic domination?

Or should we in the Name of Jesus arise and take our place as sons and daughters of God Almighty?

Col. 1:12—Conybeare Trans.: "Giving thanks to the Father who has fitted us to share the portion of the inheritance of the saints in light."

He has given us the ability to enjoy our part.

"He has delivered us out of the realm of darkness, and transplanted us into the kingdom of his beloved Son, in whom we have our redemption, the remission of our sins."

We have within us the ability of God.

We have the wisdom of God.

God is the strength of our life.

What more can we ask?

Can't you see what this means as a background for a prayer life?

Can't you hear the Spirit whispering, "Nay in all these things we are more than conquerors?"

Real prayer is inspired of the Spirit, backed up by the Living Word. Then it should be a real sharing with Him.

Col. 3:1—Conybeare Trans.: "If then ye are partakers of Christ's resurrection." Way translates it: "If then you have shared in Messiah's resurrection."

We have become not only partakers, but sharers in the resurrection ability of God.

Now He is asking us to share with Him in giving the world the message that will deliver those in bondage from the captivity of Satan.

He is calling on us to became intercessors, pray-ers, burden-bearers in this world of darkness and fear.

His Will

I saw that if I could get into the will of the Father, I would be stepping into the channel, into the current of His dream for the age.

That current would carry me on into a realm of victory and usefulness that I had never known before.

One day one of the workers said, "If we only knew where He was working, we would tie up with Him."

Another one said as he was praying, "Lord, lift us out of this little millpond where we are swimming around, out into the current of Your will for us now."

I saw it. His will was unveiled in Jesus. Jesus was His will.

Four times in the Gospel of John, Jesus said, "I came to do the Father's will; I came not to do mine own will, but the will of Him that sent me."

Can we know the Father's will?

We may know it if we know the Master.

Paul, writing to the Ephesian Church said, "Be not ignorant what the will of the Lord is."

We are not to be ignorant of it.

This Word is His will written for us.

Everything that helps men toward knowing Jesus better is in the will of the Father.

Romans 12:1-2 shows the three-fold will of the Father. "I beseech you therefore, brethren, by the mercies of God, that ye present your bodies as living sacrifices, holy, acceptable to God, which is your spiritual ministry. And be not fashioned according to this age; but be ye transfigured by the renewing of your mind, that ye may prove what is the good, and acceptable, and perfect will of God." (Lit.)

It is the renewed mind that gets to know the will of the Father.

When we are recreated, He gives us His Nature. Then He renews our minds, they walk in harmony with our recreated spirit.

As we fellowship the Word, live in it, let the Word abide in us, we get to know the good will of the Father.

We get to know the acceptable will of the Father. Then as we go on, we will get to know His perfect will. We will swing into it with an abandonment that will thrill heaven.

You say, "Mr. Kenyon, when Jesus prayed in the garden He said, not my will but thine be done."

I know. That is in the heart of every true follower of the Master. We do not want our own will. We only want His will.

We know that saving lost men is His will.

We know that carrying the Gospel to the world is His will.

We know that teaching and building up the believer is His will.

We know one hundred things that are His will. It is His will that our bills should be paid, that we should be strong and vigorous in our walk, that we should have a testimony that would make people strong to trust in Him.

The man who lives and walks in Him will never pray outside of His will.

I love to think that Jesus did the Father's will, that He taught the Father's will, and then He suffered His Father's will in His Substitutionary work.

In the Pauline Revelation, He reveals the Father's will to us. ~~Jesus, you see, was His will revealed.~~

~~As you study Jesus, you will know the Father's will.~~

Jesus' death and Substitutionary Sacrifice were the will of the Father.

~~Jesus was the will of God unveiled.~~

We Are the Father's Will

When that first came to me, how it thrilled me.

Jesus came to do the Father's will. Jesus was the Father's will, "and of His own will He brought us forth by the Word of truth."

If His own will brought us forth, we are born of His will, aren't we?

We are born of God. We are born from above. We are His will.

Say it outloud, "I ~~am the Father's will~~."

Say it until your ears become accustomed to it, until your spirit absorbs it.

"I am my Father's will. It is easy for me to do His will, for I ~~am born of it.~~ I have His nature in me. I have the impulses of His own love heart throbbing through me.

"He is love; I am born of love. I have His nature in me. That nature rules me. His love is shed abroad by the Holy Spirit in my heart. It dominates me. I love because He first loved me.

"I have come to believe in His love in my case. I believe that His love-way is the best way."

When Jesus said that He was the Way, the Reality, and the Life, that was the Love-way, and Love was the reality of that way.

That was the Father's life. That life has been imparted to us.

We are born of the Father's will, born of His love nature.

We are partakers of the divine nature.

We have the Father's Word now as it fell from the lips of Jesus. We can live in the Father's Word.

The Father's Word is His will, so we may live in His will.

"How can I do this?" you ask. Begin now to say that you are doing it. After a bit, it will become a reality to you.

~~You never rise above your confession. If you always confess your failings, your weakness, your lack of ability, your weakness and your lack of ability will rule you.~~

If you say, "I can do all things in Him who strengthens me," you will rise to the level of it.

You never enjoy anything beyond your confession. Your faith is never stronger than your confession.

If you are afraid to confess that you are the Righteousness of God in Christ, there will be an uncertainty about your actions.

You will hesitate.

If you dare say, "I am a branch of the vine, and the same life and love that flows in the vine flows in me," you will rise to the level of your confession.

If you say over and over again, "I know whatever I ask of the Father in Jesus' Name, He will give it to me," after a while that truth will permeate your consciousness until it becomes a literal, absolute fact in you.

Men and women will come to you for prayer. They have not learned the secret. They haven't any faith of their own. But they have faith in your faith, because you have learned the secret of confessing to be what God says you are.

That is all there is of it.

When you dare join hands with God, when you dare to sing the song with Him, that song will be the harmony of Heaven.

In other words, when you dare to say that you are what He says you are, then the two of you have agreed and you become a messenger of heaven, and you will be doing the works that Jesus said you should do in His Name.

Thomas has become a deified saint in the hearts of multitudes of people.

You hear them say unctiously, "I am a doubting Thomas."

They little realize what their confession means.

They have unconsciously allied themselves with the man who likely hurt Jesus from a spiritual point of view more than any other of His disciples.

Thomas' faith in the Master was based upon purely sense knowledge grounds.

He said, "When I can see the wounds in his hands, put my finger into the wound and my hand into his side, then I will believe."

I know of nothing so utterly cruel as unbelief. There has never been an armor for the heart that could shield it from the spear of unbelief.

That Roman soldier no more assuredly reached the heart of Jesus than did the unbelief of this loved man, Thomas.

Sense knowledge faith is one of the most dangerous enemies and one of the most deep-seated errors in the modern church.

The sense knowledge believer knows very little of the Pauline revelation. He lives in the realm of the senses.

He is oft-times suspicious of the man who walks in the spirit.

He is ever trying to get faith, praying for faith, but never arrives.

He knows the Bible is a Revelation from God, but he knows nothing of revelation faith.

He lives in a spiritual fog.

He is the personification of mysticism.

Chapter The Fourteenth

THE THOMAS KIND OF FAITH

I NEVER realized how many people had this kind of faith You remember the story in John 20:24-29, "But Thomas, one of the twelve, called Didymus, was not with them when Jesus came. The other disciples therefore said unto him, We have seen the Lord. But he said unto them, Except I shall see in his hands the print of the nails, and put my finger into the print of the nails, and my hand into his side, I will not believe.

"And after eight days again his disciples were within, and Thomas with them. Jesus cometh, the doors being shut, and stood in the midst, and said, Peace be unto you. Then saith he to Thomas, Reach hither thy finger, and see my hands; and reach hither thy hand, and put it into my side: and be not faithless, but believing. Thomas answered and said unto him, My Lord and my God. Jesus said unto him, Because thou has seen me hast thou believed? (marg.) Blessed are they that have not seen, and yet have believed."

This is the Thomas type of faith.

It is Sense Knowledge faith.

We can believe in miracles if we can see them.

In many healing meetings multitudes have sat in amazement when they have seen the sick instantly healed.

It has given them faith to dare ask for their own healing.

This was not faith in the Word.

It is faith in what they see and hear or feel.

We see it again manifest in an instance like this: Someone comes to me sick. They are in great pain. When I pray for them the pain leaves them instantly; and they say, "Thank God I am healed."

I ask, "How do you know you are?"

And they reply, "The pain is gone."

They have no faith in the Word. It is meaningless to them.

I read them Isaiah 53:4-5, and say, "Do you believe that?"

"Oh, yes; I have believed that for years."

I read it again: "Surely he hath borne our sickness and carried our pains; yet we did esteem him stricken, smitten of God, and afflicted." (Marg.)

"He was wounded for our transgressions, he was bruised for our iniquities: the chastisement of our peace was upon him: and by his stripes we are healed."

You see, this person is healed by my faith; or his faith in my faith.

They are like the one in James 5:14 who calls for the elders to come and pray over him and anoint him with oil, and the prayer of the elders heals him.

The only faith he had, was in the elders.

That is Sense Knowledge faith.

He can see the elders. He can hear them pray; can feel their hands upon his head.

The Word actually means nothing to him.

Had he believed the Word instead of sending for the elders or asking anyone to pray for him, he would have looked up and said, "Father, you laid this disease on Jesus, and it is unseemly for me to bear it. I dishonor Thee in bearing it. So in the Name of Jesus, I command it to leave me, and I command Satan to take it with him. I have no use for it, and I refuse to have it."

In Jesus' Name he gets his personal deliverance.

He honors the Word, and the Name.

He honors the Father and Jesus.

He has learned to take his place in Christ.

Jesus met only sense knowledge faith among the Jews.

In Matt. 8:5-13 is recorded the story of the centurion who came to Jesus beseeching Him to come and heal his servant who was sick of palsy.

And Jesus said, "I will come and heal him.

"The centurion answered, Lord, I am not worthy that thou should come under my roof; but only say the word, and my servant shall be healed."

He illustrates his confidence by saying, "I also am a man of authority, having under me soldiers: and I say to this one, Go, and he goeth; and to another, Come, and he cometh; and to my servant, Do this, and he doeth it."

When Jesus heard this He said, "I have not found so great faith, no, not in Israel."

This Gentile had faith in the Master's word that no Israelite had manifested.

In John 6:30 you catch a glimpse of the Jews' faith in Jesus. It was exactly like Thomas' faith.

"They said therefore unto him, What then doest thou for a sign, that we may see, and believe thee?"

When they saw the miracles they believed.

I question if a single one of the disciples that walked with the Master had anything but sense knowledge until after the day of Pentecost.

Luke 24:11 gives a picture of the disciples after Mary Magdalene, and Joanna, and Mary the mother of James; and the other women with them told the disciples that Jesus had risen.

"And these words appeared in their sight as idle talk; and they disbelieved them."

They couldn't believe beyond their senses.

John 6:14 gives us another illustration. "When therefore the people saw the sign which he did, they said, This is of a truth the prophet that cometh into the world."

His words filled them with wonder or with anger, but not with faith.

They had to have some physical evidence to prove His Deity.

1 John 1:1-3 also illustrates this perfectly: "That which was from the beginning, that which we have heard, that which we have seen with our eyes, that which we beheld, and our hands handled, concerning the Word of life (and the life was manifested, and we have seen, and bear witness, and declare unto you the life, the Eternal Life, which was with the Father, and was manifested unto us); that which we have seen and heard declare we unto you also, that ye also may have fellowship with us."

That which we have seen with our eyes, handled with our hands —that is in the realm of the senses.

God sent His Son down here into the realm of Sense Knowledge, and those sense knowledge folks saw Him, ate with Him, witnessed His miracles, but not one of them actually believed He was going to rise from the dead, though He had told them so.

They didn't believe that He was going to die for their sins.

They only believed what they could see, and hear.

None of the disciples believed in His resurrection until they had some physical evidence of it.

You remember the dramatic scene of Peter and John coming to the tomb finding the stone rolled away, and the empty grave clothes. John then said that he believed. (John 20:1-10)

One of the gravest dangers that we face as believers is sense knowledge faith.

The thing that He demands of us is that we accept His Word as it is, the very Word of God; and that we act upon it, independent of any feeling or any evidence that the eyes can see or the ears hear.

Have you noticed carefully Rom. 10:8-11?

"But what saith it? The word is nigh thee, in thy mouth, and

in thy heart: that is, the word of faith, which we preach: because
if thou shalt confess with thy mouth Jesus as Lord, and shalt believe in thy heart that God raised him from the dead, thou shalt be
saved: for with the heart man believeth unto righteousness; and
with the mouth confession is made unto salvation. For the scripture saith, Whosoever believeth on him shall not be put to shame."

You note He is challenging us to accept the Word that we may
have heard so many times that we know it from memory.

So He says, "The word is nigh thee, in thy mouth and in thy
heart: that is, the word of faith."

Next He demands that I confess with my lips, my faith in
the resurrection of Jesus; He demands that I confess my salvation;
and that I have become His righteousness in Christ.

I must confess this before I receive Eternal Life, before I
am recreated, before I become the righteousness of God in Him.

And He says that if I do it, I shall not be put to shame.

This is acting on the Word independent of any sense knowledge whatever.

That is faith.

For me to act when I have evidence, is not faith.

I require no faith when I have physical evidence.

You see, faith is giving substance to a thing that is not.

I am giving thanks to the Father for the money to pay the
bills before the money has arrived.

All I have is Matt. 6:32-33: "Your heavenly Father knoweth
that ye have need of all these things. But seek ye first his kingdom, and his righteousness; and all these things shall be added
unto you;" and Phil. 4:19: "My God shall supply every need of
yours."

That is all I have. That is all I ask.

And that Word has given me the assurance that I will get the
thing that I asked Him for.

Jesus said, "Whatsoever ye shall ask of the Father in my
Name he will give it you."

I have asked the Father in Jesus' Name, now I am thanking
Him that His Word cannot fail.

In another part of the book you will read a little exposition
on Phil. 4:6-7. Let me add a bit to it.

"In nothing be anxious."

Why should I be anxious?

Isn't He my Father?

Don't I know Him?

Didn't He say that He would look after my needs, and whatsoever I ask in Jesus' Name He will give to me?

Didn't He say, "He that spared not his own Son, but delivered him up for us all, how shall he not also with him freely give us all things?" (Rom. 8:32.)

How can I be otherwise than perfectly quiet?

The thing hasn't disturbed me.

For instance, suppose my child is very ill. Doctors have given it up, but that doesn't disturb me. I have His Word and I know Him. He can't fail me.

Didn't He say, "They that believe shall lay hands on the sick, and they shall recover?" (Mark 16:17-18.)

Supposing I can't get to the child, then I have this scripture: "Whatsoever ye shall ask of the Father in my Name He will give it you." (John 16:23.)

Do I need anything more?

Why He says, "I watch over my word to perform it."

"No Word from God is void of power."

Now you can understand the rest of this: "In everything by prayer and supplication with thanksgiving, let your requests be made known unto God."

Did you notice, "with thanksgiving"?

I can't help but be thankful.

I can't help but praise Him.

Why, this sickness or this impossible financial obligation simply gives Him an opportunity to reveal Himself as my Father, and Jesus as my Lord and provider.

If I didn't have that need, I would never know the riches of His grace; so I thank Him for every added burden that comes, for it gives Him an opportunity to reveal Himself to my heart.

Did you notice the next verse?

When I begin to thank Him and praise Him, "The peace of God which passeth all understanding throws a garrison of faith's soldiers around my heart, guarding it, and guarding my thoughts so that no doubt can come."

Why, I am just as quiet as God is, because God's peace has garrisoned my heart.

Did Jesus ever get disturbed?

Was He anxious when He saw the waves dashing over the little vessel in which He and the disciples were riding?

Not a bit; He simply said, "Peace, be still."

He knew that every Word He spoke was the Father's Word; and it was the Father saying through His lips, "Peace, be still," and the waves became quiet.

When the demoniac, that fierce, dangerous man, came out and intercepted them in the Gadarenes, the Father said through

Jesus' lips, "Be still; come out of Him."

And the demon said, "May we go into that herd of swine?"

Jesus answered, "Go."

Jesus was speaking the Father's Words; He wasn't excited or anxious.

He knew that what the Father said through His lips would master that demon force, or quiet that raging sea.

And that same peace of God comes into your heart that was in the heart of Jesus.

The Bitter Failure of Sense Knowledge Faith

"I think I am losing faith in God.

"I have had such strong faith. Why, I have been healed so many times. Every time that I have been sick and have asked prayer from my friends, I have been instantly healed; but now I have had ever so many pray for me and I get no relief.

"I tell you, I am beginning to lose faith."

I asked him "What are you losing faith in?"

He answered, "Faith in God, to be sure."

And I said to him, "Why you've never had any special faith in Him to lose. You've had many healings, but have you ever gone to Him for your own healing?"

"No, I've always had you people pray for me."

"Then all you have had is sense knowledge faith.

"You have trusted in other people's faith.

"You have been a spiritual hitchhiker ever since we first became acquainted.

"You have never trusted the Word for yourself.

"You have been a leaner rather than a burden-bearer.

"You have leaned on other people. You have never taken your place in Christ, and the hour has come when their faith can't carry you any longer. You must take your place yourself.

"Are you a son?"

"Oh, yes, I know I was Born Again years ago."

"But you have never grown any. You are but a babe yet.

"You live in the realm where you were when I first found you.

"You have never come out of the sense realm.

"Don't you think now that you had better begin to study the Word?

"Take our correspondence course. Get to know what you are in Christ; what belongs to you.

"Get to know your authority over sickness and disease through the Name of Jesus."

"I thank you for speaking so plainly to me. I can see where my difficulty lies, but you see I have been so busy with my business and I have been struggling so hard to make good, I guess I have failed to get the best out of life."

"No, you have just awakened, and now you will get it. It is a short road. It is only a few blocks up, and you will be rejoicing with the rest of them having your own faith, having your own place in Christ.

"You will be praying with sick folks. Men will be coming to you and saying, 'Won't you pray for me?' or, 'I wish you would pray for my child;' and, oh, the joy that will be yours."

Sense Knowledge holds one a prisoner. One is always looking for physical evidence, and as long as one does that, faith doesn't have an opportunity to exercise itself.

You pray for something. Then you must act as though you had it. You must talk as though you had it.

You are never to go back on your prayer, never to allow your lips for one moment to say that you are not certain that you have it, that you are not sure of your answer.

You remember Mark 11:24: "When ye pray, believe that ye have received; and ye shall have." That is the marginal rendering.

Then there is only one thing to do. We must begin to praise Him for it.

I remember that years ago I was praying for money to meet our rent bill. I had prayed. Then I went out on the street and I began to wonder how I could get it.

Before I realized it I had destroyed my prayer. I had nullified the Word.

I came to myself, asked for forgiveness, and then began to thank Him for it. I held myself steady and kept my heart singing songs of victory. That was the beginning of my life of prayer.

Then I remember how I grew out of that and came to the place where, when I had asked Him for something, I forgot it; I left it; I walked away from it.

If it came back to my mind, I thanked Him; I praised Him for it.

Then I learned that when someone brought the subject up, to tell him that it was settled. "I have it."

Once a man said, "If you have it, then there is no need of my helping you."

I smiled and said, "I have it according to the Word, for no word from my Father is void of fulfillment; so I praise Him as though I had it now."

One day while walking down Halsey Street in Chicago I was facing a great need. I asked Him for it in that Name, and began to praise Him for it.

It seemed as though I could feel it in my pocket. I wouldn't put my hand in to verify it, but I walked down the street hardly touching the sidewalk. My heart was full of laughter.

When I reached the house where I was called upon to pray for a sick woman, the money was handed to me. It was more than I had asked for.

"In nothing be anxious." Is He not for you? Is He not working for those who trust Him?

There is no ground for anxiety or fear if you know His Word. Whosoever believeth shall not be put to shame."

I know this to be an absolute fact.

You see, your heart will learn to welcome the impossible, the "beyond reason" task; for the Greater One is in you, with you, and for you.

Most of us have never seen the difference between Jesus' and Paul's teaching on faith.

Jesus was talking to the unregenerate Jew.

Paul is talking to the recreated sons of God.

The body of Christ is what Jesus wanted the Jews to be. He told them what faith would do.

Paul tells us what faith has made us by grace.

Jesus urged and demanded faith on the part of the faithless Jewish nation.

The Pauline Revelation lets us into the secret that we are believers; and as believers, we are possessors of all the things that Jesus promised that faith would do.

The believer has a legal right to the use of the Name of Jesus.

It is not a problem of faith with him—whatever he asks of the Father in Jesus' Name he gets.

Jesus said to the believing ones, "If two of you shall agree as touching anything that you ask of the Father, it shall be done unto you."

That didn't belong to the unregenerate Jew, it belonged to the body of Christ.

When we urge the believer to believe, we are ignoring the fact that he is a believer, and that all things belong to him.

When we take what Jesus said to the Jew about faith and try to get this untaught believer to exercise faith, we are sinning against the Pauline Revelation and the untaught believer.

What we should do is to so open the Word that he can't help but act upon it.

We should never urge the unsaved man to believe, but we should give him the Word to act upon. Believing is acting on the Word.

The man without Eternal Life can act upon the Word.

He can take Jesus Christ as his Savior.

He can confess Him as his Lord.

And the moment that he does it, God takes him to be His child and imparts to him Eternal Life; then all things in Redemption belong to him.

Chapter The Fifteenth

NEVER URGE PEOPLE TO BELIEVE

GIVE them something to act upon and they will do it.

Open the Bible to them until Acts 20:32 becomes a present tense reality. "And now I commend you to God and to the word of His grace which is able to build you up and to give you the inheritance among all them that are sanctified."

Paul is leaving the church at Ephesus. He may never see them again and he commends them to the Father. He turns them over into the hands of love.

And he said, "I not only do this, but I commend you to the word of His grace." These Epistles of Paul's are the words of His grace.

The four gospels are the words of His grace, and so the whole New Testament makes up the book of the words of the Father's grace.

If he were here he would say, "I want you to study it. I want you to prove yourself capable of doing the Word."

There will be ability in the Word as you study it to put you over and make you a conqueror.

To merely know the Word has no real value in it unless it becomes a part of your life.

It does not become a part of your life until you begin to practice it.

As you begin to live the Word, then the Word becomes a part of your very being, enters into your blood, into your very system. The very strength and ability of God becomes a part of you.

1 Cor. 2:12 has a beautiful suggestion here: "That we might know the things that were freely given to us by God."

These things that were given to us were in the finished work of Christ. We have access to all the riches of His grace unveiled in that finished work of Christ. (Read Col. 2:2-3)

Notice some of them.

Satan was conquered, defeated by Jesus before He arose from the dead, and that defeat of Satan is set to our credit so you can safely say and joyously too, "I conquered Satan in Christ."

167

As Jesus was Master of the Devil, so I am in His Name.

I was raised together with Christ.

I have in me His resurrection ability, His resurrection life. I am a Master. (Read Eph. 1:17-23)

And that great, mighty Holy Spirit who has come to make His home in my body is guiding me into all the reality of the wealth that has been given to me in Christ.

He is making me know what the resurrection means to me: that if I were raised together with Christ, I am a Master of the forces that operated in slaying Jesus; that I am now taking Jesus' place in this earth walk.

I have a legal right to the use of His Name that has all authority.

I have a legal right to the ability of the Holy Spirit and I know it is God who is at work within me, willing and working His own good pleasure. I am not left to my own resources.

2 Cor. 9:8 "And God is able to make all grace abound unto you; that ye having always all sufficiency in everything, may abound unto every good work."

God is making His grace to come leaping toward you in all its fullness, and that grace has within it His all sufficiency for every emergency.

What a Master you are!

How ashamed we ought to be that we have ever talked about our weakness and our lack when the ability of God, the measureless ability of God is ours.

Why, in the tenth verse He says, "And he that supplieth seed to the sower and bread for food, shall supply and multiply your seed for sowing, and increase the fruits of your righteousness."

How little we have appreciated this that His very sufficiency and ability are all at our disposal.

You understand what He means by "increase the fruits of your righteousness." All the gracious words that Jesus said and all the mighty acts that He performed were the fruits of His righteousness.

I wonder if we have ever thought of it.

Jesus was fearless in the presence of the enemy in every place.

He had no fear of a storm at sea.

He had no fear of lack.

He wasn't afraid of death. He raised Lazarus who had been dead four days.

He wasn't afraid of a mob.

Those were some of the fruits of His righteousness.

When these fruits abound in us they will make us like Jesus, and these fruits can abound in us.

Righteousness was given to us with that intent.

2 Cor. 4:4-5 "And such confidence have we through Christ to God-ward; not that we are sufficient of ourselves, to account anything as from ourselves; but our sufficiency is from God who also made us sufficient as ministers of a new covenant."

Now notice this carefully. He is not only our ability, but He is our sufficiency.

There is no lack in us, in our service, in our finances, in anything connected with our earth walk.

You see when He took us over and came into us and began to build His Word into us, He was building His sufficiency and His ability into us.

That Word of His created this universe; created this earth with all its flowers and fruits, its wealth of minerals, chemicals, and oils: His efficiency in that Living Word created these things.

Now He is building into us that Living Word with its supernatural efficiency.

A Prayer Life backed with this knowledge becomes invincible.

We haven't said anything but what is true in regard to the New Creation.

All we need to do now is to take our place and act our part for it is God who is at work within us.

Not only is He building Himself into us, but He is there to work through us.

Now just take this thing home to your heart and read Eph. 1:3, "Who hath blessed us with every spiritual blessing in the heavenlies in Christ."

You are blessed with everything that you need.

His very fullness is yours.

His ability is yours.

His love is yours.

Yes, He Himself is yours!

Contrast Of Paul and Jesus On Faith

Christ tells us what the Jew can be.

Paul tells the Believers what they are in Christ.

Christ tells the Jew what he could do if he had faith.

Paul tells us what we are because we have believed on Christ.

Paul reveals to us that we are in the realm with Christ now.

Jesus tells them, "If they believe."

Paul shows us that we are believers and that we possess all things in Christ.

Paul's revelation is what we can do, because we are what Jesus wished the Jews to be.

Jesus is talking to a nation of natural men.

Paul is speaking of the New Creation, the sons of God, members of the body of Christ.

Jesus is speaking to the First Covenant people who have lost their faith in God.

Paul is speaking to those who are in Christ, sons of God.

Jesus is challenging the unbelieving Jew by revealing what faith will do in the lips of a man.

Paul thanks God for leading him in triumph in Christ.

Jesus said to the disciples before Pentecost, "Greater things than these shall ye do because I go unto the Father."

All that Jesus had done for Israel was in the sense realm.

He had healed the sick.

He had fed the multitudes.

He had opened blind eyes.

He had raised the dead, and stilled the sea.

But the disciples, after they were recreated, were to perform miracles upon men's spirits.

They were to do spiritual things as well as things in the sense realm.

The "greater things," were to lead men into the New Creation and unveil spiritual realities for them to enjoy.

Jesus was surrounded by unbelief, and He was seeking to inspire faith in natural man.

It would be well for us to recognize this fact, that natural man cannot have faith in the revelation realm.

He has sense knowledge faith.

He believes what he can see, hear, and feel.

All God asks him to do is to act on the Word.

He demands that he confess Jesus as Lord and act upon the Word that declares Christ died for his sins and was raised for his justification.

For years I tried to get natural men to believe. I can see them now struggling, crying, weeping and confessing their sins. It was so hard for them to grasp it.

But now I can see how simple it is.

All I ask them to do is act upon what God has spoken, and He counts that as faith.

The man who acts on that enters into the family, becomes a member of the body of Christ.

He becomes a partaker of the divine nature, so that all things that God wrought in Christ in the Substitution belong to him.

Now he can act intelligently on the Word either for himself or for another.

Believing is acting on the Word.

Faith is the result of acting.

Under the First Covenant, the word "faith" does not occur in connection with Moses or Israel until Paul unveils it in the eleventh chapter of Hebrews.

Moses obeyed what the angel told him to do.

God never left it as a problem of faith, but it was a problem of obedience.

The word "faith" does not once occur.

They were servants acting under orders from God which came through angels.

Malachi 1:6 unveils it to us. "A son honoreth his father, and a servant his master: if then I am a father, where is mine honor? and if I am a master, where is my fear? saith Jehovah?"

Malachi 3:16: "Then they that feared Jehovah spake one to another; and Jehovah hearkened, and heard, and a book of remembrance was written before him, for them that feared Jehovah, and that thought upon his name."

And Malachi 4:2: "But unto you that fear my name shall the sun of righteousness arise with healing in its wings."

All through the Old Covenant you will notice, especially in the Psalms and in the prophetic books, that Israel feared Jehovah.

Fear and love don't blend.

They were natural men who lived under an iron law called the law of death.

We are the New Creation folks.

Fear has been taken out of us, and we love because He has imparted His love nature to us.

All of Israel's mighty men were mighty because God revealed Himself to them.

They learned to do what He told them to do.

In 1 Kings 18:36 Elijah said, "O Jehovah, the God of Abraham, of Isaac, and of Israel, let it be known this day that thou art God in Israel, and that I am thy servant, and that I have done all these things at thy word."

Then the fire fell upon the altar and consumed the offering and the altar.

Elijah was simply doing what God had told him; not through anything that he had read, but an angel always communicated with him, or God gave him a dream or a vision.

Today we are to act upon the written Word.

During the first century of the early church only a very few people had the written Word.

Wherever Paul went, it was "the spoken Word."

Where Peter and John went, it was "the spoken Word."

We have the written Word, but faith makes of it a living Word, a life giving Word, a healing Word, a comforting Word.

To the unbelieving it is just ink on paper; just words that may bring condemnation, or, if the heart is responsive, bring life and healing.

Legal and Vital Side of the Plan of Redemption

It helped me greatly when I found that prayer was based on legal grounds; that it didn't depend upon struggle and long hours of agonizing before the Lord.

It wasn't based upon pity, but upon a legal foundation.

You remember that the Bible is made up of two covenants, two contracts: The old one and the new one.

The first contract was made with Abraham—sealed with blood.

The second contract was between Jesus and the Father—sealed with the Son's blood.

Israel were the beneficiaries of that first covenant.

We are the beneficiaries of the second.

Our redemption is based on legal grounds.

Our New Birth is legal.

Every child of God is legally in the Family.

The book of Romans that gives to us the plan of Redemption is the greatest legal document in existence.

The New Testament or New Covenant is the greatest document on jurisprudence ever given man.

Heb. 7:22: "By so much also hath Jesus become the surety of a better covenant."

God said to Abraham, "By Myself have I sworn." He becomes the surety of the old covenant.

You see, the throne is back of the covenant. Jesus and the Father are back of the new covenant and prayer is based upon this covenant—consequently, it is based upon legal grounds.

Heb. 11:1—One translator makes it read: "Faith is the title deed to things hoped for, putting to the proof things not seen."

Practically all the basic terminology of English Law comes from the Bible.

Then if prayer is based on legal grounds, we should learn what they are.

In the first place, we are legally justified or made Righteous; legally Born Again; have a legal right to Eternal Life and a son's place in the Father's family.

And He is legally responsible for us because He brought us into being.

There are two phases of our Redemption: One is the legal and the other is the vital.

The legal is what God has done for us in the past, like the substitutionary sacrifice of Christ.

The vital is what the Holy Spirit through the Word is doing in us.

Rom. 4:25 is a good illustration of the legal: "Who was delivered up on account of our trespasses and was raised for our justification."

The vital is illustrated in Phil. 2:13: "For it is God who is at work within you willing and working His own good pleasure." Also 2 Cor. 5:17.

Eph. 3:16-19: "That he would grant you according to the riches of his glory, that ye may be strengthened with his ability through the spirit in the inward man, that Christ may dwell in your hearts on the ground of faith; to the end that ye being rooted and grounded in love, may be strong to grasp with all the saints what is the breadth and length and height and depth, and to know the love of Christ which passeth knowledge, that ye may be filled unto all the fulness of God." This is vital.

Notice the next verse: "Now unto him that is able to do exceedingly abundantly above all that we can ask or think according to the ability of God that is at work within us."

Redemption is legal. It is in the past. It is a finished work.

The New Birth is vital. It is now.

When you know that prayer is based on legal grounds and you know that God has legally tied Himself, has bound Himself to do certain things, then you will learn to take your place and act accordingly.

His Son, the Living Word, is the guarantor, and gives you your rights and privileges in Redemption.

God gave us this Word of His own free will.

He has led us into the prayer life.

He has led us to trust Him and now He will not fail us.

So we can confidently turn to Isaiah 41:10 and hear Him whisper: "Fear thou not for I am with thee; be not dismayed for I am thy (Father) God; I will strengthen thee; yea, I will help thee; yea, I will uphold thee with the right hand of my righteousness."

That "right hand" is Jesus and He is upholding us by the Word of His power, by the Word of His grace.

The reader will notice some new expressions in this book, and perhaps many new translations of the Word.

One expression that you will meet again and again, is "Sense Knowledge."

You know that all the knowledge that natural man has, has come to him through the five senses: seeing, hearing, tasting, smelling, and feeling.

His knowledge has come to him through these five avenues.

We know the result if one was born blind, the sense of color would have no meaning; if born totally deaf, music would mean nothing to him.

There is another kind of knowledge with which we are dealing in this book. This is Revelation Knowledge from the Word.

It is knowledge that comes through our spirits and reaches our intellect.

The faith problem is a spiritual problem.

Faith and love both come from the human spirit.

We contact God with our spirits, not with our reasoning faculties.

No one can find God except through his spirit.

No one can know God except through his spirit.

This is the reason that sense knowledge men in the scholastic world repudiate the Bible; because sense-governed reason cannot understand the Bible or its author.

One must receive God's nature before spiritual things become intelligible.

Chapter The Sixteenth

CASTING DOWN REASONINGS

THE battle of faith is with Sense Knowledge reasonings. Man's word has been at war with God's word ever since the beginning in the Garden.

The real struggle today that every believer must wage is with Sense Knowledge that governs the human race.

"But I say, Walk by the Spirit, and ye shall not fulfill the desires of the senses. For the senses war against the spirit, and the spirit against the senses; for these are contrary the one to the other; that ye may not do the things that ye would." It is our re-created spirits. (Gal. 5:16-18 Lit. Trans.)

We may talk about faith in man, faith in ourselves, faith in the works of man without opposition; but when we talk about having faith in the Bible, in the Word of God, we often find rebellion.

You will find that Sense Knowledge is faith's worst enemy.

It will never give the Word first place. It admires the Word, but does not obey it.

It often confesses it as God's Word, but obeys man's words.

As I look over the books that fashioned my early Christian life, I note that almost everyone of them was written to prove that the Bible agreed with the latest dictum of Science, that man's word had more authority than the Word of God.

Having been mentally trained in Sense Knowledge, I found it difficult to give Sense Knowledge a second place, and the Word of God its real place.

"Fight the good fight of faith, lay hold on the life eternal (realities) whereunto thou wast called, and didst confess the good confession in the sight of many witnesses." (1 Tim. 6:12)

In the fight of faith, there is but one weapon, the sword of the Spirit.

The combat is with reason which is governed by the Adversary, through the senses.

The Adversary is like the political boss in our great cities. His name is seldom ever mentioned. He is a hidden force. He puts up puppets to do his will.

Satan uses the same tactics. He has given us a fetish, called Science.

How fearful I was of Science in my early days. I did not want to appear unscientific.

What is Science? It is the knowledge that has been gathered through years of hard study by sense knowledge ruled men.

Through Science has come most of our knowledge. It has been gained by experimentation and by observation. How men have worked and sacrificed to get this knowledge. We honor them for their achievements.

Sense knowledge comes from the five senses. The body is the laboratory. The contacts it makes with material things are carried to the brain by the sensory nerves, which divides and classifies it.

It has no other means of knowledge.

Sense knowledge cannot go beyond things it has seen, felt, heard, tasted, or smelled. Whenever it leaves these avenues, it goes into the realm of speculation, of theory, trusting that the theories may become realities in the next step of the experiment.

Darwin had nothing but theories and guesses when it came to the question of Creation.

As long as he could see or handle things, he was working on quite sure ground. But when he was asked the reason for Creation, the reason for Man, the source of Life and Gravitation, he had but a guess.

We may clothe that guess in the most beautiful language, but it is only a hypothesis at best.

Faith deals with facts. The Word of God has no speculations, no theories, just declarations of fact.

Eph. 6:4-18 gives a picture of our spiritual warfare. We are to put on the whole armor. "Stand therefore, having girded your loins with truth, and having put on the breastplate of righteousness, and having shod your feet with the preparation of the gospel of peace." Our shield is faith, our sword is the Word of God.

Every part of this armor is put on by faith. The whole armor in which we are garmented is a faith armor.

You cannot see Truth, you cannot see Righteousness, you cannot see Peace, you cannot see Faith.

You cannot feel or hear any of them. Their substance is all in the spirit.

When we come to recognize that spiritual things are as real as physical things, then we will be able to understand the background of the faith life.

Heb. 4:14: "Let us hold fast to our confession." Our confession has not one physical thing in it. It hasn't anything that can be seen, or felt or heard, outside of the Word of God.

Faith is not based upon reason nor upon things that men can see unless the thing they see is the Word of God.

1 Cor. 2:5: "That your faith should not stand in the wisdom of men, but in the ability of God."

The wisdom of which He is speaking is Sense Knowledge wisdom.

"We speak of wisdom, however, among them that are full-grown: yet a wisdom not of this world, nor of the rulers of this world, who are coming to nought." This is God's wisdom.

One translation reads: "Yet not a wisdom of this world, nor of the de-throned powers of this world."

Jesus dethroned the powers that govern sense knowledge.

Nowhere does Paul make it as clear as he does in 2 Cor. 10:3-5: "For though we walk in the flesh, we do not war according to the flesh." (or senses)

Though we live in the realm of the Senses, we do not war with the weapons of the Senses.

"For the weapons of our warfare are not of the Senses, but mighty before God to the casting down of strongholds."

What are the strongholds?

"Casting down imaginations, and every high thing that is exalted against the knowledge of God (or Word of God); and bringing every thought into captivity to the obedience of Christ."

We cast down reasonings, for men have deified reasonings. The great reasoners of the world and the great philosophers of the world have gained the ascendency over the human mind.

The philosopher is the apologist for the failure of the Sense Knowledge man.

No man turns philosopher until he has the sense of utter failure, and he is writing an excuse for that failure.

Philosophy has never given anything of any value to the church.

What we called our Christian philosophers are often men who denied the miraculous and the supernatural.

They denied that God could hear prayer and would heal men today.

Philosophy is the swan song of human failure; it is born of the senses.

We are to cast down imaginations or reasonings, everything that sense knowledge has exalted against the Word of God, and we are to bring into captivity our thinking so we will think God's thoughts instead of man's thoughts, so we will be inspired by the Word of God rather than by the word of man.

God is a faith God. It took many years to find this out. I could think of Him as a love God, a holy God, an omnipotent God, but to think of Him as a faith God was revolutionary.

There are two scriptures that we should notice.

Heb. 11:1: "Now faith is the substance of things hoped for, a conviction of things not seen," or "a reality of things not seen."

Another translation: "Now faith is the title deed to things we have hoped for."

You never expect anything Now, for which you hope. Hope is always in the future.

There is nothing firm, or solid or tangible about hope. But faith gives reality to this thing you have hoped for, that you never would have had otherwise.

Rom. 4:17: "Before him whom he believed, even God, who giveth life to the dead, and calleth the things that are not, as though they were." God calls the things that are not, as though they were, and they become.

Speaking of Abraham He said, "Who in hope believed against hope, to the end that he might become a father of many nations, according to that which had been spoken."

This is a striking scripture. Abraham had a battle with hope. Finally he arrived. He believed against hope. He counted God's word to be absolute.

"Without being weakened in faith he considered his own body now as good as dead (he being about a hundred years old), and the deadness of Sarah's womb; yet, looking unto the promise of God, he wavered not through unbelief, but waxed strong through faith giving glory to God, and being fully assured that what he had promised, he was able also to perform." Rom. 4:19-20.

Abraham looked at his body and saw it exactly as it was, impotent, a worn out thing.

He looked at Sarah, another broken vessel. Yet looking unto the promise of God, he waxed strong. He counted that God could make good what He had promised.

Abraham moved into God's class. He counted the things that were not as though they were, and they became.

He counted his body to be as good as it was at the age of thirty-five years. He considered Sarah to be as young, and capable of bearing children.

He counted the thing that was not as though it was, and it became.

Reason would have conquered had he yielded to it. Reason said, "Tradition shows that no man has ever had his youth renewed, that no woman past ninety years of age has ever had a child."

Yet this man believed against all the evidences of Sense Knowledge; and counted that God was able to make good what He had promised.

Heb. 11:3: "By faith we understand that the worlds have been framed by the word of God, so that what is seen hath not been made out of things which appear."

God had said before, "Let there be an earth," and the earth came into being.

He said, "Let there be light." It was not the light of the sun or moon. It was a light that gave us the sub-tropic heat during the first four days of creation, that gave us our vast fields of coal and oil. There was no rotation of the earth, thus the whole of it was sub-tropic.

All that God did to create the universe was to say, "Let there be light in the firmament of heaven to give light upon the earth," and the sun, moon, and stars came into being.

The sun and moon did not function until the beginning of the fifth or sixth day. It would take ages on ages for the light to come to the earth from the distant stars.

God's only machinery for creation was His Word. In that Word was the faith of God expressed.

It is a strange thing that we have not been taught that our words can be filled with either faith or unbelief, or cold speculation; we have not realized their effect on the hearer!

It is our words that build up great organizations and institutions.

It is our words that destroy or build. It is words that are filled with faith or unbelief.

Faith words are constructive. The man who inspires faith is a builder. He is constructive.

The man who inspires unbelief is an enemy of progress. Faith is giving substance to the Word of God.

It is giving substance to things we have hoped for.

Faith makes man God-like, just as love makes him God-like.

God is a faith God, and when man links up with God, he becomes a faith man.

He and God work together, and walk together.

2 Cor. 5:7: "We walk by faith, and not by sight."

The believer is a faith person. He does not walk by reason. He does not walk by Sense Knowledge.

He lives and walks in the realm of faith.

Eph. 2:8-10: "For by grace have ye been saved through faith; and that not of yourselves, it is the gift of God; not of works, that no man should glory. For we are his workmanship, created in Christ Jesus for good works, which God afore prepared that we should walk in them."

It is by grace we are saved. It is through faith. It is not of man's works. It is the gift of God. It is not of works lest any man should boast.

The New Creation comes into being purely on the ground of faith.

God first believed it into being. Now we believe that Creator Being (Holy Spirit) into us. Our whole struggle in the faith life is to take the Word of God instead of the word of man—to rest in God's Word rather than in man's word.

My Resources

It staggered me when I said out loud, "God is the fount of my Resources because He is the strength of my life; He is my ability; He is the Author and substance of my faith."

I am a partaker of the Divine Nature. "These things have I written unto you that ye may know that ye have eternal life, even unto you that believe on the name of the Son of God."

His Life is His Nature.

His Nature is Love.

If I have His Nature I have a measure of His ability. I have a measure of His Love.

His wisdom is given to me in Christ without measure, so I can safely say that He is my ability.

You remember that Jesus said to the disciples, "Tarry ye in Jerusalem until you receive power from on high." (Luke 24:49)

The word "power" comes from the Greek word "dunamis." Young translates this "ability," and it is a better word. They were to tarry in Jerusalem until they received the ability of God.

You not only received the Nature of God, but when the Spirit came into your life you had in you the ability of God, the very Resources of Heaven.

No one yet knows the limit of that ability.

It must be exhaustless.

Col. 2:9-10 gives us a suggestion. "For in him dwelleth all the fulness of the Godhead bodily, and in him ye are made complete or full, who is the head of all principality and power."

Take with that Gal. 2:20, "For it is no longer I that live, but Christ liveth in me."

He has come into me in all His fulness.

He has come into me with all His completeness.

Now we can understand John 1:16: "Of his fulness have we all received, and grace upon grace."

The Limitless One has come into me to take me over.

He gave to me His ability, His completeness.

Now I can understand Col. 1:9. Here is Paul's prayer: "I do not cease to pray and make request for you, that ye may be filled with the exact knowledge of his will in all spiritual wisdom and understanding."

The Greek word translated "knowledge" is "epiginosis," which means "complete, perfect, or exact knowledge."

It means the very fulness of His ability.

1 Cor. 1:30 says God has made Jesus to be Wisdom unto us.

Wisdom is the ability to use knowledge to my advantage.

I have the knowledge of the complete and perfect Substitutionary Work of Jesus.

Now I have the ability to incorporate that knowlege in my daily life.

I have spiritual wisdom and understanding so that I may walk worthily of the Lord, unto all pleasing, bearing fruit unto every good work and continually increasing in this exact, this perfect knowledge of God. (Col. 1:9-13)

I am made powerful with His ability, according to the might of His glory.

I now have steadfastness and longsuffering because of what I am in Christ.

I do not chide or condemn myself.

I throw myself open to this new life, this new unveiling of what I am in Christ.

I am longsuffering with those who can't see it, who seem to be unable to take it in, as I was once.

In the meantime, with great joy I am giving thanks unto the Father who has given me this ability to enjoy my share of the inheritance of the saints in light; for "I have been delivered out of the authority of darkness and translated into the kingdom of the Son of His love; in whom I have my redemption from Satan's thralldom."

This new light has given me a new responsibility in the prayer life.

I can understand now why He said, "Come boldly unto the Throne of Grace" into the Throne Room where He and the Father are seated together.

I am not to come as a servant or a slave, but I am to come as a Lover, a Son.

But prayer is not going to be what it was before I knew who I was, and what my privileges were.

Now I am going in to sit with Him in the Council Room. I am going to call His attention to the needs of the brethren who are sitting in the darkness of sense knowledge, while they pray for faith and seek for power.

I am going to find out how they can be helped to see the Light of Life, for I remember the Master said in John 8:12, "I am the light of the world: he that followeth me shall not walk in the darkness, but shall have the light of life."

I have found that Light of Life.

I am no longer walking in the darkness of sense knowledge.

I am no longer crippled by my inferiority complex or my sense of unworthiness.

I know that I am a son beloved; that I have my place in the Father's presence.

When we come to understand love's intimacy, love's privileges, love's right to the Father's ear, we may rush into his presence at any time without an apology and lay our needs before Him—not only our personal needs, but the needs of those about us.

We can enjoy the ability and wisdom of our Father, and we will go out with that strange, sweet fragrance that is found only in the Throne Room, a fragrance that will cling to our garments.

Yes, our very words will have in them Love's own sweet fragrance.

Men will know that we have been with Jesus, have been in fellowship with Him.

I said to a young man, "What are you doing here?"

He said, "I am helping the Father train these young men and women how to act upon the Word, how to allow the Word to dwell in them and gain the ascendency over them."

I asked, "Then you are one of the Father's helpers, are you?"

He replied, "Yes, I am sharing with the Father. I have given Him my ability and my training, and He is giving me His wisdom, His grace and love, and we are laboring together to build up this body of believers."

That young man had caught the vision.

He was a sharer with the Father and with the Master.

We are to be laborers together with Him.

We are God's husbandmen.

We are God's tilled land.

We are God's fellow-workers.

We sow His seed. He waters it and makes it grow.

We open the Word and give it, and He makes it fruitful in the lives.

We are bearing up under the load of the Master in the Salvation of a lost world.

I wonder if it has ever occurred to you that you could become one of the Lord's inner circle helpers; one that could enter the throne room anytime and sit in counsel with Him.

Many of us in our prayer life are simply praying at Him, talking about Him, talking about the Word rather than feeding the people with the Word.

The preacher really is like a mother who eats and then feeds the child at her breast.

We are to give sincere milk of the Word. That milk can only come from the heart-life of the teacher.

Until the preacher has assimilated it, until it has become a part of his life, he cannot nurse the congregation.

We assimilate it only in the measure that it abides in us.

We feed upon it. We live in it. We live on it. It rules us. It is the voice of our Master.

Then when we teach, we bring the sincere milk from the very heart of our Father to the hungry, needy ones that listen.

Chapter The Seventeenth

FELLOWSHIPPING THE FATHER

F GOD is for you, who can be against you? He that spared not his own Son, but delivered him up for us all, how shall he not with him freely give us all things?" Rom. 8:31-32.

God and you are working together in carrying out His dream for the Redemption of the world.

He can't get along without you, any more than you can get along without Him.

Jesus' illustration of the vine and the branches perfectly illustrates this. The vine can't bear fruit without the branches and the branches can't live without the vine.

Now you can understand the next verse: "Who shall lay anything to the charge of God's elect? It is God that has made them righteous; who is he that condemneth?"

Not the Master, and He is the only one who has the legal right to do it.

This is a part of the conclusion of the first eight chapters of Romans. It shows the absolute oneness of the Father and His children and of their perfect fellowship and cooperation with the Father. It also shows their mastery over the forces of darkness and circumstances.

He climaxes it with, "Nay, in all these things we are more than conquerors."

This is the background for a prayer life.

We have little groups of people who are making prayer a business. They are intercessors.

One group takes the requests for prayers that come in through the mail from our Correspondence Course and our books.

They have become experts in prayer.

They are getting the things that are being requested.

You see, God is active on your part.

He is standing up for you.

He is fighting for you.

He is supplying your needs.

Out of the treasury of His grace He is giving you His Wisdom and Ability.

2 Cor. 3:4-6 likely has become very precious to you: "And such confidence have we through Christ to God-ward: not that we are sufficient of ourselves, to account anything as from ourselves; but our sufficiency is from God; who has made us sufficient as ministers of a new covenant."

You see we aren't common folks.

We are tied up with Omnipotence.

We are united with God Himself.

We are carrying out His will here on the earth.

We are the channels through which He is pouring Himself upon the world.

So it is perfectly normal that He should become our sufficiency. That His ability should become our ability.

Limitlessness of Prayer

Now we can understand a Scripture we have used before; "Laboring together with Him."

This is fellowship with the Father. He is supplying strength and grace and ability to the intercessor.

It is working with all wisdom and ability.

Now you can understand Col. 1:9-12 (Lit. Tran.): "We do not cease to pray and make request for you that ye may be filled with the exact knowledge of his will in all spiritual wisdom and understanding."

This word "knowledge" as some of you remember, is "epiginosis."

This is something that He is supplying to you who are entering the prayer life.

It is a perfect knowledge of His will.

You can't make a success of the prayer life unless you know His will; unless you have His own wisdom and understanding, you are going to fail.

No matter how much you pray, your prayers will not be effective until you know His will.

1 John 5:14-15: "And this is the boldness which we have toward him, that if we ask anything according to his will, he heareth us; and if we know that he heareth us whatsoever we ask we know that we have the petitions which we have asked of him."

That settles the issue.

If we are in His will, our prayers are heard and answered and we get the thing for which we are praying.

So it is necessary that we have this perfect knowledge of His will for our prayer ministry, in order to "walk worthily of the

Lord unto all pleasing, bearing fruit unto every good work and increasing in this exact knowledge of God."

We are thinking of a prayer fruit now.

Jesus illustrated that. John 15:7-8: If ye abide in me and my words have found their place in you, ye shall demand your rights and they shall come into being. Herein is my Father glorified that ye bear much fruit."

That translation is very precious to me. He lets me see my legal standing and rights, now I can go to the Father and get the thing that my neighbor or brother needs.

When they send a handkerchief to us to pray over, we know that our prayer is going to bear fruit, that the request is granted when I pray.

You see, this is not walking in darkness.

This is having an "exact knowledge of His will in all spiritual understanding."

This is moving up into the realm of the recreated spirit where you fellowship with Him who raised Jesus from the dead.

You learn to pray for the thing that He wishes accomplished.

You are in the groove, the current of His will.

You become His "Mike." He speaks through you.

You are His transmitter, His willing instrument through which His will can be done.

What He wishes done is done. You see that His will is carried out.

He can cast out demons through your lips now.

He can heal the sick through your lips. Your lips become His transmitter.

The Word in your lips is a living thing.

The Name in your lips becomes Omnipotence.

You take His place and do His work.

You have His "all authority" that was given to Him after He arose from the dead.

It thrills you, doesn't it?

You have His ability: that is Love's ability.

You will love even as He loved.

His Nature, that love nature fills you.

His Name is like a checkbook with a limitless account in the bank.

His Word, who can describe it?

The heart melts as it contemplates it.

His Word!

It is the Master speaking: "In my name ye shall ask what ye will and it shall be done unto you."

His Word is the sword of the spirit, one moment slaying un-belief and doubts and fears. The next moment it is the sweet force of love to heal the broken-hearted, give courage and strength to the weak.

His Word in your lips is like the Father's Word in Jesus' lips. It defeats the forces of darkness.

It strengthens those whom Satan has made weak.

I hardly dare give you the next sentence: His Word in your lips makes you a superman.

You have all authority over the power of the Enemy.

It is love that has been delegated to you.

It is love pouring itself through your lips.

You can enter the throne room at will. You are always wel-come.

You are master of the laws of nature that would hurt and hinder.

You stand quiet in the presence of humanity's needs knowing that you have authority to open the flood gates of grace, of life and love and let them pour over the wounded broken-hearted men and women struggling in life's uneven fight.

Sharing With Him

The highest order of prayer is a love affair: two lovers meet-ing, sharing with each other.

Not slaves and the master; neither servants and an overlord; but a Father and His children.

We come together as suggested in Matt. 18:19-20: "Where two or three are gathered together in my name, there am I in the midst of them. If two of you shall agree on earth as touching anything they shall ask of the Father, it shall be done for them."

This is not talking at Him. Much praying is merely talking at the Father.

This is a meeting together. Jesus said, "There am I in the midst of them."

It is a business meeting. It is a meeting in loving council.

You speak telling your needs, then wait listening for Him to bring to you the Word of assurance.

The highest order of prayer is a dialogue: you and He con-versing about His work.

You are there to talk things over with Him.

You are a son taking a son's place.

You are not conscious of your standing or righteousness.

You are intent upon doing His will, carrying out His will.

You and He are working together.

You see, He has made you not only a New Creation and a Son, but He has made you a partner in this work.

You are the fruit-bearing part of the company.

You are the hands and feet and the voice of the company.

Oft-times you are asking for another—one of His children is in distress, and you are asking His cooperation and His ability to meet that distress.

One of His children has been injured in an accident and you are coming to Him for healing for the injured one, and for strength and courage for the loved ones.

You know your place in Christ and you are taking it now boldly.

You have gone beyond the period when you think of faith or your ability to stand in His presence. That is all of the past.

You know what you are in Christ, and you are assuming the responsibilities that belong to you.

You Are Making a Business Of This Prayer Life

You and He have gone into business together. He has furnished the capital and the wisdom: you furnish your ability and time and talents, with His blessing upon them.

You recognize the gravity of it. It is an eternal thing; you are dealing with eternal issues, and eternal spirits.

You are doing business with Him to carry out His will in the redemptive work that was wrought through Christ.

You realize that He cannot work without human aid. Angels can't do the work, nor any other heavenly being.

It devolves upon us, and you are taking your place as a junior member of the firm.

You are His contact man.

It may be that you are in the ministry, or a layman, or an official in some organization. You are taking your place now, representing Him.

You are bringing to Him the needs of your friends.

He is bringing to you the assurance that He will meet the needs.

The Seated Christ

Jesus did not sit down at the right hand of the Majesty on high until He had finished the work of Redemption.

Some of the outstanding features of this Redemption are His absolute mastery over Satan. He dethroned the Adversary. He stripped him of his authority and power.

And you understand that in that substitutionary work of Christ, we were identified with Him.

The Spirit makes it clear in Gal. 2:20: "I have been crucified with Christ."

The old version is "I am crucified," which is incorrect.

In Col. 2:12: "Having been buried with him in baptism, wherein ye were also raised with him through faith in the working of God, who raised him from the dead."

Not only were we crucified with Him, but we died with Him.

We were buried with Him.

We suffered with Him.

We were justified with Him.

We were made alive with Him.

We conquered Satan and stripped him of his authority, with Him.

And then Eph. 2:5-6: "Made us alive together with Christ, and raised us up with him, and made us to sit with him in the heavenlies."

Not only were we made alive and raised, but in the mind of Justice we are seated with Him today.

What does that mean?

It means absolute dominion over our enemies.

It means utter oneness with Christ. As the branch and vine are one, so are the individual and Christ one.

His victory was our victory.

His mastery over the forces of darkness was our mastery.

And so when He sat down, He entered into His rest, for His work was finished.

When we understand, we enter into His rest with Him.

Then we have entered into our rest. Our days of want, of fear, of anxiety are over. "We have cast all our anxiety upon him for He careth for us."

So if Jesus is seated, His work is finished.

All we do when we accept Him as our savior is enter into the benefits of that work which He has done for us.

We are healed the moment we say, "Surely he hath borne our pains and carried our sicknesses; yet we did esteem him stricken, smitten of God, and afflicted (with our diseases);" and our anxiety ends and our healing becomes real.

"My God shall supply every need of yours." The fear of want ends.

We have entered into our rest with Him.

Of His Fulness

John 1:16: "Of his fulness have we all received and grace upon grace."

Col. 2:9-10: "For in him dwelleth all the fulness of the Godhead bodily, and in him ye are made full or complete who is the head of all principality and power."

Another wonderful Scripture, Eph. 1:22-23: "And he put all things in subjection under his feet, and gave him to be head over all things to the church, which is his body, the fulness of him that filleth all in all."

Again, Eph. 3:19: "And to know the love of Christ which passeth knowledge, that ye may be filled to all the fulness of God."

What is this fulness?

Col. 2:2-3 may help us. Here is Paul's prayer for the Colossian believers: "That their hearts may be comforted, they being knit together in love, and unto all riches of the full assurance of understanding, that they may know the mystery of God, even Christ, in whom are all the treasures of wisdom and knowledge hidden."

Then all the fulness and riches that belong to the believer, that were purchased for us in Christ's great substitutionary sacrifice, are in Christ.

"Of his fulness have we all received." Every believer has received a portion of that fulness, that completeness.

Among the great treasures of this fulness is His love nature. Everyone of us has received Eternal Life, the nature of the Father, and that nature is love.

1 John 4:16: "For God is love."

We have never majored this fact that we were a love product, that we are begotten of love, that we have received the love nature; and we have never realized that we have in us the greatest thing in the world.

1 Cor. 13:13 declares: "Now abideth faith, hope, and love, these three: and the greatest of these is love."

It is the greatest because it is the nature of God.

One stands mute in the presence of a fact like this, that we have in us God's nature.

The thing that hurts is that we have never given that nature sway. We have held His nature in bondage. God has been a prisoner in us.

Paul was no more a prisoner in Rome than the Holy Spirit has been a prisoner in us.

The second greatest thing that comes to us in the New Birth is joy.

This is something that makes trouble lose its grip upon us; makes poverty lose its terror.

It is the Joy of the Lord.

And you remember that He said, "The joy of the Lord shall be your strength." That was a prophecy.

Now Jesus said, "My joy I give unto you."

You understand the difference between joy and happiness. Happiness depends on the things that we have or own, like property or loved ones. But joy is a thing of the spirit. It is the one quality that has made Christianity attractive to the world.

Joy is an artesian well in the spirit that bubbles up, overflows. It is the thing that Jesus said the Holy Spirit would give us.

John 7:38: "He that believeth on me, as the scripture said, from within him shall flow rivers of living water, (or shall gush forth torrents of living water)."

This is joy unhindered, pouring out from us with a joyous spontaneity that attracts at once and captivates.

A person is speaking on the street, holding a meeting, and his voice is filled with a contagion. It grips the hearts of careless hearers. They draw near and listen. "Out from his inner life is gushing torrents of living water," and living water is full of divine laughter. "It is joy unspeakable and full of glory.

1 Peter 1:8: "Whom not having seen ye love; on whom, though now you see him not, yet believing, ye rejoice greatly with joy unspeakable and full of glory." This is the attractive feature of the divine life.

Another one of the fruits of His fulness is "peace that passeth all understanding."

It moves up out of the realm of the senses into the realm of the spirit.

No matter what the persecutions may be, peace like a river flows through the spirit.

No matter what the turmoil is around, the peace of God rules.

Jesus said, "My peace I give unto you." That is one of the most outstanding features of the divine life.

He said, "Her face shone with a heavenly joy and her spirit seemed to be held captive by a peace that passed understanding." They were talking of a martyr that had been bound to the stake. Joy in the midst of death, and peace in the midst of agony.

This fulness not only has love, joy, and peace, but all the fruits of the recreated spirit seen in Gal. 5:22.

"Of his fulness have we all received." It doesn't belong to just a few, but it belongs to every believer.

The successful prayer life is one of self-denial. It is a recognition of His Lordship, a giving up of much that is not wrong in itself but that hinders and takes our time.

A prayer life doesn't mean hours spent in actual prayer, but hours of study and meditation in the Word until the life becomes literally absorbed in the Word and the Word becomes a very part of us.

One could spend hours in prayer fruitlessly if the heart is not prepared beforehand.

The preparation of the heart comes from meditation in the Word, meditation on what we are in Christ, what He is to us, and what the Holy Spirit can mean to a life that becomes God-inside minded.

Prayer is fellowship with the Father and with Jesus, a cultivation of a habit of communion. It is learning to take advantage of our rights in Christ. It is assuming the responsibility that those rights give us.

Prayer privilege means prayer responsibility.

Chapter The Eighteenth

WHAT HE IS TO US

WE know what He was to Israel under Moses in the four books of the law. We know what He was to Israel under the leadership of Joshua. We know what He was to Israel during all the years of their walking under the Covenant. No enemies could stand before them.

We know that under David, Israel conquered the entire inhabited world, and in all their wars never was there a soldier slain unless Israel had broken the Covenant.

If He was that to Israel and they were but servants, what could He be to us, His sons and daughters.

Isaiah 48:13: "Yea, my hand hath laid the foundation of the earth, and my right hand has spread out the heavens: when I call unto them, they stand up together."

Notice that expression. "When I call them, they stand up together."

God's voice controls the universe.

And remember that when the Man of Galilee spoke to the sea in the midst of the storm it became calm and quiet in a moment.

Every law of nature was obedient to that man.

We stand in the presence of creative faith, God's creative ability.

You can hear Him say, "When I call they come into being."

Things that were not become.

In Romans 4:17, speaking of Abraham, Paul said: "Before him whom he believed, even God, who giveth life to the dead, and calleth the things that are not, as though they were." And they become.

It thrills the heart when we realize what our Omnipotent God of Love and Father is. "He called into being what does not exist" is the way Moffat translates it.

That is dominating faith; that is creative faith.

In Matt. 14:13-21 is a story of Jesus feeding the multitude. He took in His hands five small loaves and two fish and He blessed them. He broke the bread and fed five thousand men beside women

195

and children. After the meal was over, they gathered up twelve basketsful.

In this story we are given two facts. First, Jesus ruled the law of supply and demand by ruling the very laws of nature.

Second, the twelve basketsful they collected showed that He not only met their need, but over and above. It was beyond all that they could ask or think.

That is our Christ. How proud we should be of Him. How we should brag about Him before men. He is our Lord.

If we had a son or father or relative that could do such miracles, we would brag about him.

He is our Lord. He is our Saviour.

We are partakers of His nature. Don't you remember, "I am the vine and ye are the branches"?

How utterly one we are with Him! How we should rejoice in the fact that we have such oneness.

We read in John 5:25-29: "The hour cometh, and now is, when the dead shall hear the voice of the Son of God; and they that hear shall live. For as the Father hath life in himself, even so gave he to the Son also to have life in himself. Marvel not at this: for the hour cometh, in which all that are in the tombs shall hear his voice, and shall come forth."

That is our Master, our Lord.

That is dominating, creative faith.

Romans 4:19-21 gives us a picture of Abraham's creative faith. Read this story over carefully until your spirit catches fire.

"And without being weakened in faith he considered his own body now as good as dead (he being about a hundred years old), and the deadness of Sarah's womb; yet, looking unto the promise of God, he wavered not through unbelief, but waxed strong through faith, giving glory to God, and being fully assured that what he had promised, he was able also to perform."

Abraham was a Blood Covenant friend of Jehovah. That Blood Covenant was sealed with the blood of an animal and the blood of Abraham mingled.

Our Covenant is sealed with the Blood of Jesus Christ. Deity and humanity united in the Incarnation.

How much better is the Blood of Jesus Christ than the blood of an animal!

How much better is the life of the Son of God than the life of a mere man like Abraham!

We are bound to Him by an indissoluble Covenant. He is bound to us as Jehovah was bound to Abraham in that Covenant.

If Abraham, a friend of God, could accept an angel's testimony and act upon it, what can we as sons of God do? You know what happened to Abraham. His youth was renewed. Sarah's youth and beauty were renewed so that a king fell in love with her, not knowing that she was Abraham's wife, and wished to marry her. She was past ninety years of age, and the following year she gave birth to Isaac.

That was the God with Whom you and I are dealing. He is our Father.

If Abraham could accept the testimony of an angel, can't we accept the testimony of the New Covenant? We have become the very sons and daughters of God Almighty.

By a new creation, we are partakers of His very nature. We have become heirs of God, joint heirs with Jesus Christ. We are the next of kin to the Son of God. How it thrills the heart!

And you understand in another chapter I have shown you that Jesus has given us the power of attorney to use His name.

When the Master was ready to leave the earth to go back to the Father He said: "All authority hath been given unto me, in heaven and on earth; go ye therefore and make disciples of all the nations, teaching them to observe all I commanded you: and lo, I am with you always, even unto the end of the world."

We have never taught them to observe or to do all that He commanded.

Didn't He command them with love's commandment to love one another, even as He had loved; to bear one another's burdens as He bore ours; to lay hands on the sick and to cast out demons in His name?

Can't you see what it meant when He said, "Lo, I am with you always, even unto the end of the age?"

If we would use that Name with the authority invested in it, we could break the power of Satan over our loved ones; we could heal the sick. Instead of there being just one George Mueller caring for thousands of little orphans by faith, there would be thousands of men and women whose prayers would feed and clothe the needy and the hungry.

We have never taken the Word seriously. We have never acted as though it were true.

If someone wrote you a letter and told you that he had deposited five thousand dollars to your account in the bank to take care of your bills, and if you knew that he was financially able to do it, you would not hesitate a moment. You could hardly wait to get to the bank. You would hand the letter to the cashier with confidence. You know the man who wrote the letter; you know the promise he made; you know the money is there waiting for you.

Is the Word of your Father, the Word of the Master to be depended upon as the word of a friend?

What a background is this for faith! What a prayer life can grow out of truth like this!

You can see what He is to us and what we are to Him.

Nothing is impossible to Him, and all His ability is ours.

What an opportunity to bless and help by our prayers!

God's Word

When the angel visited Mary to tell her the glad tidings of the Father's will for her to be the mother of the Incarnate One, she said a remarkable thing. Luke 1:38: "Behold, the handmaid of the Lord; be it unto me according to thy Word."

How that grips the heart! Hear her say, "Behold, here am I; your love slave. Be it unto me, Oh Lord, according to thy Word."

What sublime confidence that Jewish maid had in the word of that angel when she said this.

Previously she had spoken, "How can it be? I am not a married woman."

The angel replied, "The Holy Spirit shall come upon thee, and the power of the Most High shall overshadow thee: wherefore also the holy thing which is begotten shall be called the Son of God."

And then the angel said these words: "For no word from God shall be void of power."

We have two other translations:

"Nothing is impossible to the word of God," and "With God nothing shall be impossible."

This is creative ability. This is God's word.

How it thrills our hearts when we realize that God and His Word are one. Mary recognized that God and His Word were one. God's Word is God's faith expressed. It is God's confession about Himself. His Word is invested with God's authority and God's ability.

You remember that He said, "By the Word of God were the heavens made."

Heb. 11:3: "By faith we understand the worlds have been framed by the Word of God so that what is seen hath not been made out of the things which appear."

That is faith's creative ability through words.

You remember that practically all of Jesus' miracles were performed with words. He said this significant thing: "The words that I speak unto you are not mine, but the Father's who sent me."

In John 12:49 we read: "For I spake not for myself, but the Father that sent me, he has given me a commandment, what I should say and what I should speak."

So Jesus was not using His own words, but the Father's words. The words that have come down to us spoken by the Master were the words of the Father. They were creative words; they were healing words; they were demon-dominating words: words filled with God and His faith.

I have been thrilled lately by noticing the faith of Jesus. He believed that He could redeem men if He became sin and suffered in their stead. He believed that if He conquered Satan, that men would accept that victory as their own.

He believed that if He arose from the dead, that men would believe that He was the very Son of God. He believed in the merits of His finished work; that men could stand in His presence without condemnation.

He believed that He could take these old, broken, wrecked human beings and recreate them and make them the very sons and daughters of God.

He believed that He could take this wreck of a human that had been dominated by sickness and sin through the ages and make him a new creation; make him to dominate the devil and circumstances and make him master where he had served as a slave.

Jesus believed in Himself, in what He did. He believed that men would respond to it and would accept it and would receive Eternal Life, the Nature of the Father. They would then become worthy sons and daughters of God Almighty.

The Word can't lie. It is a part of God Himself.

We act on the Word. God will make it good.

What a foundation is this for a prayer life!

We have God's own Word to back us. No Word from God can fail.

We can have real assurance in our prayer. When we pray in Jesus' Name, it is as though He prayed. It is answered.

Some Facts About the Believer

The believer is a child of God, a new creation. His spirit has been recreated. He has come into the family of God. He is in the realm of the supernatural. He is in perfect union with the Master.

The believer and Jesus are one. He is the head and they are the body; so He says: "All things are possible to him that believeth."

That means to a believing one—one who has come into the family of God, who has become a new creation created in Christ Jesus.

This is not a hyperbole; this is just a statement of fact. Just as all things were possible with Jesus, all things are possible to the believer through the Name of Jesus.

You remember that in 1 John 4:4 it reads: "Ye are of God, my little children, and have overcome them (speaking of demoniacal forces) because greater is he that is in you than he that is in the world."

You grasp it. Your heart knows it. You are of God, born from above.

God Himself recreated you, imparted to your spirit His own Nature. Now you stand before Him as though you had never been weak, as though you had never been a failure, as though you had never been under condemnation. Again He says, "Nothing shall be impossible unto you."

This is to the man of faith.

This is the man created out of righteousness and holiness of truth. He is talking about the one that He came to recreate, this new man.

Of him He says: "There is now no condemnation to you because you are in Christ Jesus."

There is a perfect union of your spirit with His spirit. You are His representative here on earth.

He says that we are ambassadors on behalf of Christ. An ambassador is an empowered representative of a country where his citizenship is located.

You are born of Heaven; your citizenship is there. You have received your credentials from heaven.

God is your actual Father. You are His child.

Your Lord and Master has told you that all authority has been given unto Him in Heaven and on earth. "Go ye therefore and make disciples of the nations."

Don't forget to teach them all that I have commanded you.

That is a mighty ministry.

In John 14:12-14 we read: "He that believeth on me, the works that I do, shall he do also; and greater works than these shall he do because I go unto the Father."

He went unto the Father to become the Mediator, Intercessor, Saviour, Advocate, and Lord of the Church. He is now at the right hand of the Father. He is going to enable us to take His place and do the same kind of works that He did before He went away.

In the next verse He gives us the power of attorney to use His name: "Whatsoever ye ask in my name, that will I do." "If ye ask anything in my name; that will I do."

This is not prayer to the Father.

This is dealing with demoniacal forces as illustrated in Acts 3 where we see the man lying at the Beautiful Gate of the temple, evidently with infantile paralysis. "And Peter, fastening his eyes upon him said, 'Look on us.'" "In the name of Jesus of Nazareth, walk."

In that Name, he broke the dominion of Satan over the man.

That man had believed in sickness, weakness, and he was helpless.

The Name of Jesus broke the dominion of faith in disease and weakness and in its place gave perfect healing and a new faith in health.

Notice again, "Whatsoever ye shall ask in my name." That word, "ask," in the Greek is "demand."

Whatsoever ye shall demand in my name, I shall make good."

We are coming into the realm of the supernatural where we see ourselves as representatives of Omnipotence and where we have an opportunity to draw on Omnipotence to meet Satan in open combat.

John 15:7: "If ye abide in me and my words abide in you, ye shall ask what ye will and it shall be done unto you."

That lets us into the realm of cooperation with the Father.

We are taking Jesus' place here on earth; we are acting in His stead. We are doing the work that He began to do.

He came to destroy the works of the adversary.

We are continuing that work of destruction.

We are His co-laborers, working under His direction, setting man free from the dominion of the black prince.

You see, the believer is united with all authority, all ability.

You remember that Jesus said in Acts 1:8 just before His ascension: "But ye shall receive power when the Holy Spirit has come upon you and ye shall be my witnesses."

The word, "power," comes from the Greek word, "dunamis", which means ability.

"You have the ability to use my name and cast out demons and heal the sick, deliver men from the bondage of want into the liberty wherewith I have made you free.

"You have the ability to understand me and to make me known.

"You have the ability to understand the revelation that I am going to give through my love-slave, Paul."

Ability means wisdom. Wisdom is ability to use knowledge and to handle circumstances and take advantage of opportunities.

The believer has the very Nature of God. God is love.

We are born of love. We are a love creation.

We have the ability to love even as He loved.

We have the ability to know men and to be able to meet their need and to help them.

You see, the believer has God in him. "For it is God who is at work within you, willing and working his own good pleasure."

How limitless becomes our ministry when we realize the integrity of the Word, when we know we have what He says we have, when we know we are what He says we are, when we know we can do what He says we can do!

We step out of the narrow limits of theology and sense knowledge into the boundless ability of God.

Now we understand what it means when we say, "I can do all things in Him who strengtheneth me."

With quiet confidence we face the impossible, knowing that He is Master.

You understand that we never pray for anything we can do ourselves or that we can accomplish ourselves.

We are asking God to enable us to do the impossible.

That makes us world conquerors.

We know that greater is He that is in us than any opposition that can confront us.

Our sufficiency is of God who has made us sufficient as ministers of a New Covenant.

What courage it puts into one to know that he has God's Sufficiency.

One translator says, "He makes us sufficient for anything." So with boundless confidence we swing free in this glorious ministry into which He has called us—the ministry of prayer.

You have seen what you are in Christ, now take your place as a prayer warrior. Make hell fear you. Make heaven glad. Fill hearts of men with joy witnessing your winning prayer life.

Healing the sick is His will. Saving the lost is His will. Breaking Satan's dominion over men is His will.

Praying for ministers and missionaries is His will. Pray for this literature we are sending out that men will take their places as they know the Word.

Now swing free in your prayer life. Be big! Honor the Word. Dare to do exploits for Him.

So Shall My Word Be

We are going to take a trip now amid some of the mighty scriptures, mostly from the Old Testament. It will be like a trip into the Redwoods of California where you stand in the presence of those mighty trees lifting their proud heads up toward the clouds.

Numbers 23:19: "God is not a man, that he should lie, or the son of man, that he should repent: hath he said, and will he not do it? Or hath he spoken, and will not make it good?"

This gets into the blood. This gives us a warrior spirit. This makes you confident of your place in Christ.

This makes you know that you are what He says you are and that you can do what He says you can do.

The Word of our God shall stand forever, and you are trusting in that Word.

Your confidence is in that Word that cannot be broken.

We think of the hills and their steadfastness and yet you know the day will come when they will stop being.

"But the Word that I speak unto you", said Jesus, "Shall never pass away."

Isaiah 55:11: "So shall my word be that goeth forth out of my mouth: it shall not return unto me void, but it shall accomplish that which I please, and it shall prosper in the thing whereto I sent it."

You feel like David must have felt when he said, "I can leap over a troop."

You become by this study a master of circumstances.

The 20th Century translates Philippians 4:11: "For I have learned that in whatsoever state I am, therein to be independent of circumstances."

You see, when you get tied up with God, when you and God become identified as you do in the new creation, you pass out of the realm of the "I can't" into the realm of "I can." You are no longer a failure. You know that you can do all things in Him who strengtheneth you.

Jer. 1:12: "I watch over my Word to perform it." This is the American Revision.

How many hard places this has bridged! Impassable gulfs have become level roads to us when we realized that God was watching over His Word.

We take His Word and carry it into His presence and repeat it and say, "Father, this is what you said."

We would not say that we knew that He kept His Word. That is an insult.

We just look up and say, "Father, I thank you."

Did you ever notice Heb. 6:18: "That by two immutable things in which it is impossible for God to lie, we may have a strong encouragement."

We see all that Christianity has builded in Europe the last three hundred years disintegrating; just melting under the terrific onslaught of Satanic forces through dictators with their selfish ambitions, and yet we turn back to the Living Word with confidence.

We are dealing with Him who cannot lie.

The dictators are liars; they are the sons of the old liar, the destroyer of the whole inherited earth.

You see, "He abideth faithful; he cannot deny himself."

No word from God can ever be defaulted. There never can be any denying of His own Word.

We did not ask Him to write the Word, nor to see that it was preserved for us.

He did that; He has encouraged us to trust Him.

We would never walk by faith if He had not inveigled us, enticed us to walk that pleasant road.

We would never have depended on prayer, nor rested on His Word unless He had challenged us with love's own challenge.

Isaiah 45:23: "By myself have I sworn."

God's throne is back of this. This is repeating what He said to Abraham.

I wonder if our hearts can take it.

God is throwing a cable about the throne, dropping the cable over for us to grasp.

He said, "Do you see, I am putting my throne as surety for my Word. My very Self is enwrapped in this." Then we remember Heb. 7:22 where He says that Jesus hath become the surety of the New Covenant.

Now we have the Father and Jesus and the Throne back of every word.

If that Word should fail, it would dethrone God. It cannot fail.

God cannot be separated from His Word.

Every Word of God abides.

The word of man is as grass, but the Word of God lives on through the ages.

This Word is like God.

Now you can understand John 1:1-3: "In the beginning was the Word, and the Word was with God, and the Word was God. The same was in the beginning with God. All things are made through the Word and without the Word was not anything made that has been made."

That Word is the Creator and the creative element of the universe.

You remember in Heb. 4:12-13 it says: "It is with the Word we have to do."

We contact God through the Word. God contacts us through the Word. We act on the Word.

Now arise in your prayer life. Take the place God has given you. Set men free; heal the sick; save the lost. You can do it.

As the Father Sees Us

What assurance it gives to the heart when we come to know that the Father loves us even as He loved Jesus, that He is vitally interested in us as He was in His Son when He walked the earth.

You know that the four gospels are Jesus introducing the Father, and the epistles are the Father introducing Jesus and what He did. They also introduce the sons and daughters of God to the world.

The Church and Jesus are one. He is the Head of the body.

In Col. 1:18 we read, "And He is the head of the body, the church; who is the beginning, the firstborn from the dead."

Jesus was the first person ever born again. He was born twice. He was born of the virgin Mary; then on the cross He was made sin with our sin, as our Substitute. Then after He had satisfied the claims of justice, He was justified in spirit, made righteous in spirit, and made alive in spirit. This was the new birth.

That is the reason that you have in Acts 13:33: "Thou art my Son, this day have I begotten thee," speaking of the resurrection of the Lord Jesus.

This scripture wonderfully helped me to understand the substitutionary work of Jesus. He had actually become sin, was forsaken of God, a curse because He had hung upon the tree. After meeting every demand of justice, He was born again out of death, recreated and becomes a partaker of Eternal Life.

Now He is called the firstborn out of death, the Head of the New Creation.

You know that Eph. 2:10 says: "For we are his workmanship, created in Christ Jesus for good works."

It was that morning when Jesus was recreated that the whole church by faith came into being. In reality it began on the Day of Pentecost and it has continued until now.

So I want you to see yourself as the Father sees you in Christ. As He sees us by faith, He is able to make us by grace. As we walk in love, we are being transformed into His image.

One of the most graphic pictures is given in John's gospel. John 1:16: "For of his fulness have we all received, and grace upon grace."

His fulness here means His ability, His love, His righteousness, His utter completeness, and we have received it.

I used to wonder why He said, "And grace upon grace." Now my heart can understand it.

I shrank back and said, "Lord, it cannot be possible that I have received this fulness."

And just as you would give a fainting one a drink of water, He gave me a drink of grace, and it strengthened me to look again. I saw myself in Christ and I saw myself receiving of His fulness and His grace, of His love life and wisdom, of His very being and substance.

I could hardly understand it, and said: "Lord, it is too much."

Then He gave me another taste of His grace as it were.

I arose up and said, "It is true, I am a branch of the vine; I am a partaker of the Divine Nature."

As we act on the Word, the Word reacts in us; is built into us and so we grow up in Christ. We are partakers of His Nature, of His very substance and Being.

In Eph. 1:3 it says, "He has blessed us with every spiritual blessing in the heavenlies in Christ."

I wondered what He meant—that He had blessed us with every spiritual blessing. Something kept saying, "You are blessed. You are rich; you have His fulness. All that He is, you have."

My spirit seemed to be numb and could not take it in, and then in His great grace He seemed to enfold me, breathe into my spirit His own Life.

I said, "Yes, Lord, I am what you say I am."

And the Father has told me that I am in the beloved.

Why love marked us out for the position of sons way back berore the morning stars sang their first anthem, and we are made unto the praise of His glory. He planned that we should be holy and without blemish before Him. He marked us out for the position of sons through Jesus Christ unto Himself; and you are the marked one.

You remember in Mal. 3:17: "They shall be mine, saith Jehovah of hosts, even mine own possession, in the day that I make; and I will spare them as a man spareth his own son that serveth him."

The Father sees us as His own righteousness in Christ Jesus. For a long time that bothered me.

In 2 Cor. 5:21: "Him who knew no sin he made to be sin on our behalf; that we might become the righteousness of God in him."

I said, "I cannot understand, Lord, how you can make me as your righteousness; but you say you have, and because you said it, I accept it."

In Col. 2:9,10 He says that we are complete in Him.

You see, righteousness gives us the ability to stand in His presence without the sense of guilt or inferiority, and this completeness is the over and "above all that we can ask or think" or desire.

It is the measure filled full, shaken down, and running over. It is the Father's love for me.

I want you to see one other picture.

Jesus said, "If a man love me, he will keep my word, and the Father and I will love him and come and make our home with him."

That is a Christian home. That is living with the Father and Jesus. The Father and Jesus make themselves one with us. That is just like His Incarnation, where He came and made Himself one with man.

In the New Birth, He makes us one with Himself; and when He makes us one with Himself, He comes and lives with us.

Now you know what you are in Christ. You see your vast responsibility.

You can pray for you know how.

Read our book, "Jesus the Healer," and our book, "The Two Kinds of Faith." Then take your place in Christ.

Dare to act your part.

Dare to let God use you.

Dare to let Love reign in your life.

Dare to be in your daily life what He says you are.

Dare to *do* what He says you can do.

Dare to confess that you are what He says you are!

All is yours. Use it.

The Relation of Love to Prayer

God is love.

We are the sons of love.

Love gave us birth.

Love planned our redemption. Love consummated it in a new creation and then Jesus gave them the New Law.

John 13:34-35: "A new commandment I give unto you, that ye love one another: even as I have loved you, that ye also love one another. By this shall all men know that ye are my disciples, if ye have love one to another."

This New Law is to govern the walk of the church, the sons of God.

Jesus set an example of how we should walk, and then in the New Birth, He gave us the ability to walk even as He walked. He does not ask us to do a thing that cannot be done.

You understand that we have the nature of God, Eternal Life. The very substance of God has come into our spirits.

We have been redeemed out of the hand of the enemy; we have been translated into the kingdom of the Son of His Love in whom we have our Redemption.

Not only are we new creations, but we have become the very righteousness of God in Christ.

This gives us boldness in the Father's presence and it gives us fearlessness in the presence of the enemy or any of his works.

Then He gave to us the legal right to the use of His name so that we can rule over the adversary. He has made us masters of demons. How little we have appreciated it.

We are in God's family. God is our Father, we are His very sons and daughters.

We are to walk in love. Love is to govern our conversation; our conduct toward one another.

When we step out of love into selfishness, we break fellowship with love.

No one can walk in selfishness and pray the prayer of faith.

1 John 3:16-21 gives us a graphic picture of the relation of love to answered prayer.

"Hereby know we love, because he laid down his life for us: and we ought to lay down our lives for the brethren. But whoso hath the world's goods, and beholdeth his brother in need, and shutteth up his compassion from him, how doth the love of God abide in him? My little children, let us not love in word, neither with the tongue; but in deed and truth. Hereby shall ye know that we are of the truth, and shall assure our heart before him: because if our heart condemn us, God is greater than our heart, and knoweth all things. Beloved, if our heart condemn us not, we have boldness toward God."

In the fourteenth verse, it says, "We know that we have passed out of death into life, because we love the brethren. He that loveth not abideth in death."

"Whosoever hates his brother is a murderer and ye know that no murderer has eternal life abiding in him."

This is putting the case very clearly.

We have passed out of the realm of Satanic union, spiritual death, into the union of eternal life and love.

Jesus laid down His life for us.

Now "Love" says, "that we ought to live for the brethren," and then He says that remarkable thing, "But whoso hath the world's goods, and beholdeth his brother in need, and shutteth up his compassion for him, how doth the love of God abide in him?"

The world's goods are the things that we prize most highly, land, houses, bonds, stocks, money and beautiful things.

We have taken Satan's appraisal of their value.

These world things have made us selfish.

This new kind of love is to break the monoply of selfishness and establish a new order of life.

This new man is no longer to live unto himself, but is to give his life for others.

If he shuts up his compassion from his brother and refuses to bear his burdens and pay his bills; he at once sins against love and God says, "How does the new kind of love abide in him."

Unless we walk in love and have yielded to the lordship of love, God cannot manifest Himself through us.

The ability of God is realized only in love's freedom to act.

Selfishness imprisons love.

"My little children, let us not love in word, neither with the tongue, but in deed and in truth", or reality.

He wants us to be Love's truth doers.

You remember in Matt. 7:24-25 Jesus said, "Every one therefore that heareth these words of mine, and doeth them, shall be likened unto a wise man, who built his house upon the rock; and the rain descended, and the floods came, and the winds blew, and beat upon that house; and it fell not; for it was founded upon the rock".

You remember that James speaking says: "But be ye doers of the word and not hearers only, deluding your own selves."

This lover is a doer of love. He lives in the love realm. It is not the old Phileo love, but the new kind of love that Jesus brought, "Agapa", and so we love in deed and in reality.

Hereby shall we know that we are of the truth and persuade our hearts when we stand before Him in prayer.

If you walk in love, you can walk into the Father's presence just as Jesus did, and know that your prayers will be answered.

There is no problem of faith to confront us; you are walking in love; you are doing the word; you are letting Jesus live His life in you.

The Father can see Jesus in us; feeling Jesus in our petitions for others. He says, "If our heart condemn us, God is greater than our heart and knoweth all things."

Your heart is your spirit.

Your hearts know whether you are practicing love towards men. If they need clothes and you are able to give them, and they cannot get them, then it is up to you to meet that need. You are to treat them as Jesus has treated you. He died for you; you live for them.

Hear this: "Beloved, if our heart condemn us not, we have boldness toward God, and whatsoever we ask, we receive of Him because we are walking in love." We will do the things that are pleasing in His sight.

It makes no difference how many promises you plead, if you are not walking in love, your prayer life will be a failure.

Many people have come to me for prayer when they were sick and I have prayed for them and obtained no results. When I asked them why my prayers were not answered, they confessed that they had bitterness in their heart toward someone. The moment that bitterness was taken away, they were perfectly well.

The 23rd verse is worthy of much meditation. This is the commandment, "That we should believe in the name of His Son, Jesus Christ and love one another."

If you have not understood what it means to believe in the name, another chapter will explain it to you fully.

It is enough to know that He has given us the legal right to the use of His name, and then He tells us, "All authority has been given unto me in Heaven and in earth." He gives us a legal right to use this "All authority."

Do you remember 1 John 5:14-15, "And this is the boldness which we have towards Him, that if we ask anything according to His will, He heareth us."

If we walk in love, we never pray out of His will, and if we know that He heareth us, whatsoever we ask, we know that we have the petitions we ask of Him.

This leads us right into the heart of the Father. Now we can understand Heb. 4:16, "Let us therefore draw near with boldness to the throne of grace, that we may receive mercy and find grace to help in time of need."

This love life permits us to walk into the very presence of the Father. You may go into the throne room and stand in His presence and make your petitions known in that name, and as sure as you do, that petition is heard.

You see we have become doers of love; we were doers of selfishness. We have consented to the dethroning of sense knowledge that has reigned in us. These five senses of hearing, seeing, tasting, smelling, feeling have ruled us. In other words, our physical bodies have sat upon the throne of our lives. Now we are crowning our spirits, or to put it more clearly, we are recognizing the lordship of Jesus Christ and crowning Him as Lord of our whole being.

It was a wonderful day when love dethroned greed and love was crowned in the hearts of the New Creation.

Here are three love scenes in the book of Acts.

Few of us have realized what it must have meant to the Father to have love take over a group of men and women as it did in that upper room on the Day of Pentecost.

Acts 2:43-47, "And fear came down upon every soul: and many wonders and signs were done through the apostles. And all that believed were together, and had all things in common; and they sold their possessions and goods, and parted them to all, according as any man had need. And day by day, continuing steadfastly with one accord in the temple, and breaking bread at home, they took their food with gladness and singleness of heart, praising God, and having favor with all people. And the Lord added to them day by day those that were saved."

Here is a picture of outpoured love in the recreated men and women, and all that believed were together and had all things in common.

Those selfish Jews that had lived to make money, in a single instant have dethroned greed and crowned love as the Lord of their lives. It is a record of love at work salvaging wrecked humanity.

Satan is dethroned; selfishness and greed meet their death stroke. The Father's love nature is taking control of men in Jerusalem. They have yielded to the lordship of love.

You remember that Jesus said, Luke 24:49, "But tarry ye in the city until ye be clothed with power from on High" and in Acts 1:8, "Ye shall receive power when the Holy Spirit is come upon you." The Greek word translated "power" means ability. See how it reads: Tarry in Jerusalem until you receive ability from on High. God's own ability. These disciples had received God's ability.

Already they had performed many wonders and signs, but the mightiest of them all was when they had all things in common and no man said that what he possessed was his own. That was the miracle of miracles, "And they sold their possessions and goods and parted them to all, according as anyone had need." Here is love gaining the mastery.

Acts 4:32-35, "And the multitude of them that believed were of one heart and soul: and not one of them said that aught of the things which he possessed was his own; but they had all things in common. And with great power gave the apostles their witness of the resurrection of the Lord Jesus: and great grace was upon them all. For neither was there among them any that lacked: for as many as were possessors of lands or houses, sold them, and brought the prices of the things that were sold and laid them at the apostles' feet; and distribution was made unto each, according as any one had need."

We have another thrilling picture, "And the multitude of them that believed were of one heart and one soul." Not one of them said that aught of the things which he possessed was his own, but they had all things in common.

You have wanted to see God really work haven't you? Well if you can get a group of men and women together who will love like this, you will see the power of God, because the next verse says, "And with great power gave the apostles their witness of the resurrection of the Lord Jesus and great grace was upon them all."

Of all the miracles from the Incarnation of Jesus to His being seated on the throne, there is no miracle greater than this. This is a real Recreation. This is a picture of the sons of God letting love loose in them.

You remember Phil. 2:13, "For it is God who is at work within you, willing and working his own good pleasure."

God is love.

Then it could read, "For it is love which is at work within you."

When love is really let loose, given freedom, then miracles follow.

I John 4:4, "Ye are of God, my little children", or "Ye are of love, for God is love, and have overcome them." Why? "Because greater is love in you than selfishness and hatred and jealousy around about you."

If you would say it over, I am in love. Love reigns in me. God and I have become one in love. Now His love life is pouring through me, blessing and helping men.

What a wonderful outburst of love it was following the Day of Pentecost, but Acts 5:1-11 comes like a flash of destruction and everybody is hurt.

"But a certain man named Ananias with Sapphira his wife, sold a possession, and kept back part of the price, his wife also being privy to it, and brought a certain part, and laid it at the apostles' feet. But Peter said, Ananias why hath Satan filled thy heart to lie to the Holy Spirit, and to keep back part of the price of the land? While it remained, did it not remain thine own? And after it was sold, was it not in thy power? How is it that thou hast conceived this thing in thy heart, thou hast not lied unto men, but unto God. And Ananias hearing these words fell down and gave up the ghost: and great fear came upon all that heard it. And the young men arose and wrapped him round, and they carried him out and buried him. And it was about the space of three hours after, when his wife, not knowing what was done, came in. And

Peter answered unto her, tell me whether ye sold the land for so much. And she said, Yea, for so much. But Peter said unto her, how is it that ye have agreed together to try the Spirit of the Lord? Behold, the feet of them that have buried thy husband are at the door, and they shall carry thee out. And she fell down immediately at his feet, and gave up the ghost, and the young men came in and found her dead, and they carried her out and buried her by her husband. And great fear came upon the whole church, and upon all that heard these things."

Men and women had been selling their goods and bringing the money, laying it at the apostles' feet. No one had asked them to do it. They did it of their own free will. Love had gained the ascendancy and they were practicing what Jesus began to teach.

I wonder if you have seen in these chapters the relation of giving to answered prayer. I wonder if you have seen the relation of giving to love. No other sins are mentioned in this connection. Just one: they had lied about their giving. They pretended to give more than they gave and judgment came upon them.

It is a very solemn warning to everyone of us. We say Lord, I have given my all and we have kept back a part of the price.

When you recognize the lordship of love, it takes in all that you are, all that you are able to do and all that you are able to be. It takes in your ability, plus God's ability. It takes in your ability to bless and help humanity.

We have never given love its place in the ministry of the Word. We have never made men see what it would mean to transgress the love law and step out of love into selfishness.

What produces the highest type of faith, has been the problem of my life. I have made it my one aim to find this coveted treasure.

I have missed much that others have enjoyed in order to achieve this knowledge.

I would rather know this, and enter into its fulness than any other thing in all the world.

This book is the product of that passion in my spirit.

Here are a few facts.

Through the Pauline Revelation you may become acquainted with your Father—not merely be introduced to Him, not merely sit in His presence for a little while—but go and live with Him.

Get so that your spirit is sensitive to His desires.

If you live with a loved one, and it is a love union and a love walk, you are very sensitive to the things that the loved one enjoys and desires.

Now you begin to live with the Father and the Master until after awhile you will say as Jesus did, "I know my Father."

You will say, "I know my Master. I am getting to know what the Holy Spirit desires and loves most. I am learning to walk in the spirit; that is, in my recreated spirit.

"I am walking in the light of the life of God in my spirit.

"I am visiting with the Father almost continuously."

That is the secret of faith.

You haven't any consciousness of faith or the lack of it.

You have a desire to please Him.

You have a consciousness of what He wants to do through you to help others.

He and you are walking together.

Jesus said, "I am the way, the reality and the life."

That life is a love life; that way is a love way; and we are walking through life with Him, loving and helping people.

Chapter The Nineteenth

WHAT PRODUCES THE HIGHEST TYPE OF FAITH?

NE who read part of this manuscript said, "What is the object of this book?"

I answered by asking him a question: "What do you think the object is?"

He said, "To produce faith."

Here are a few things that have been covered in other parts of this book, but I want to bring them together so that you may intelligently check up in your own life and settle some great issues for yourself.

The first thing that is necessary is to know the integrity of the Word; to know that this Word is actually what it declares itself to be—a Revelation from God to us.

We should know that it is God speaking to us; that it is not only a Book of the past and future, but it is a Book of Now; that it is a God-breathed, a God-indwelt, a God-inspired message.

Secondly, it is necessary for us to know the actual reality of our Redemption in Christ—not as a doctrine, not as a philosophy, but as an actual redemption out of the authority of Satan, and that we have been, by the New Birth, translated into the kingdom of the Son of His love; or in other words, into the very Family of God.

Satan's dominion over us as a New Creation is ended. Jesus is the Lord and head of this new body.

Satan is a defeated foe over whom we reign through the Name of Jesus.

Satan has lost his dominion over our bodies, over our minds, over our finances, over the circumstances of life.

When we know this, as we know that four and four are eight, the problem of faith will never bother us.

Next, it is necessary for us to know the reality of the New Creation; to know the legal side of it, that in the mind of Justice we were created in Christ Jesus when He was recreated after He had been made Sin as our Substitute.

We should know that vitally, the moment we accepted Jesus Christ as our Savior and confessed Him as our Lord, God recreated us, made the legal thing a reality, and that we have today in our spirits the very Nature and Life of God.

It is not an experience.

It is not a religion.

It is not joining a church.

But it is an actual Birth of our spirits. We are the very sons and daughters of God Almighty.

We know this thing just as we know hunger and its satisfaction; as we know heat and cold.

We know that we have passed out of Satan's dominion, spiritual death, into the realm of Life through Jesus Christ.

We know it!

What will be the effect of this knowledge?

Why, God is your very Father and you are His very Child.

You have as much freedom in His fellowship as Jesus had in His earth walk, and the Father loves you even as He loved Jesus.

A fourth fact: We know the reality of our Righteousness in Christ.

There is no theory about this.

We know that Rom. 3:26 is a reality: "That he might himself be righteous and the righteousness of him that hath faith in Jesus." (Marg.)

God the Father became our Righteousness when He imparted to us His own nature, Eternal Life, in the New Creation.

Jesus became our Righteousness the moment we took Him as our Savior and confessed Him as our Lord.

He then became our Sponsor, our Lord, our Head, our very Life.

But in that great revelation, 2 Cor. 5:21, the Holy Spirit through Paul says, "Him who knew no sin God made to be sin; that we might become the righteousness of God in Him."

Not only is Jesus our Righteousness, and the Father our Righteousness, but we have become "the Righteousness of God in Him."

This means that our standing before the throne is a standing sponsored by God himself and by His Son; by His own works wrought in us, by the Holy Spirit, through the Word.

We are what He says we are.

This means we can stand in His presence without any sense of guilt, condemnation, or inferiority.

This means that the prayer problem is settled. We are no longer going into His presence tongue-tied because of condemnation or fear-filled because of ignorance.

We know what we are in Christ.

We know that He made us what we are.

It is not a problem of feeling or a problem of faith.

This does not require faith any more than Jesus required faith to go into the presence of His Father.

Jesus was—and we are.

Fifth, it is necessary for us to know the reality of Indwelling.

Of all the mighty truths connected with Redemption, this is the climax: that God Himself, after He has recreated us, made us His own, is actually making our bodies His home.

No longer does He dwell in an earth-made holy of holies. Our bodies have become His temples.

1 Cor. 6:19-20: "Know ye not that your body is the temple of the Holy Spirit which is in you, which ye have from God? and ye are not your own; ye are bought with a price: glorify God therefore in your body."

That didn't seem possible to me. What a vision I caught of what we are in Christ!

When one becomes God-inside minded, when he takes for granted that "greater is He that is in him than he that is in the world," he goes out and faces life's problems with the sense of a conqueror.

This is almost an unknown practice in the church for men and women to say in every crisis of their life, "I am a conqueror; I am more than a victor, because the Creator dwells in me. He can put me over. He can make me a success. I can't fail."

What effect will this knowledge, put into practice daily, have upon the prayer life?

Rom. 8:26 then can be a reality: "And in like manner the Spirit also helpeth our infirmity: for we know not how to pray as we ought; but the Spirit Himself maketh intercession for us with groanings which cannot be uttered."

Really, that will solve the prayer problem.

If the Holy Spirit is voicing the desires of the Father through your lips, those desires will be met and granted.

Next it is necessary for us to know the reality of our Fellowship with the Father.

This is the very heart reason for Redemption.

I Cor. 1:9: "God is faithful, through whom ye were called into the fellowship of His Son Jesus Christ our Lord."

Fellowship means sharing, equally bearing the burden, sharing in the victories; and He has called us to share with His Son.

In 1 John 1:3-4, and 7, it tells us that we may have fellowship with one another, "Yea, and our fellowship is with the Father, and with his Son Jesus Christ." We have the joy of walking in the light as He is in the light.

The highest honor He has ever conferred upon us is to be joint-fellowshippers with Himself, with His Son, and with the Holy Spirit in carrying out His dream for Redemption of the human race.

Relationship without fellowship is an insipid, tasteless thing.

It is like marriage without love or fellowship.

Fellowship is the very mother of faith, the parent of joy, the source of victory; and He has called us individually into fellowship with His Son.

If you have fellowship with Him and if you are walking in the light as He is in the light, prayer becomes one of the sweetest privileges, one of the greatest assets that we have fallen heir to in Christ.

Again, it is necessary for us to know the authority of the Name of Jesus; not as a part of a creed or a doctrine, but to know it as an actual reality; just as though some wealthy man should give to you the power of attorney to use his name—a limitless power of attorney.

What would it mean to you? And what effect would it have if he said to you in that legal document, "Supply every one of your needs, act as though this fortune were your own?"

The Father has given to us the power of attorney to use the Name of Jesus, and that Name has all authority in heaven and on earth.

That makes us absolute masters of Satanic forces.

"In my name ye shall cast out demons; ye shall lay hands on the sick and they shall recover; whatsoever ye shall ask of the Father in my name He will give it you."

That is limitless.

It is the limitlessness of the prayer life, and it belongs to every child of God.

It is not a problem of faith; but a problem of knowing your legal rights in Christ, and then taking your place as a son and daughter and actually playing the game with Him.

LAST WORDS

You have read the book.

Your honest heart has been deeply affected.

You have discovered treasures that you never knew existed.

You have found your rights and privileges in a Prayer Life.

Now what are you going to do with this knowledge?

You remember that knowledge brings responsibility; and if we do not assume the responsibility, it brings judgment.

You know too much now, not to act upon this knowledge.

Begin a Prayer Life of your own; then bring together little groups and teach them this Prayer Life.

You can do it.

You see, Prayer is a most vital and necessary thing to know about as a believer.

We shall be glad to help you in any way possible. We would be pleased to hear from you. Write while the glow is upon you.

Inspiring Books by E. W. KENYON